IN THE WORD *WITH MICHELE TELFER*

God's Grace

Through the Ages

12 STUDIES IN THE OLD AND NEW TESTAMENTS

Published by:
Michele Telfer Ministries PO Box 19142
Newbury Park, CA 91319

www.InTheWord.com

ISBN 979-8-9893254-0-5

Printed in the United States of America

For my dear friend Karen Stimer,
whom God used to make this happen

TABLE OF CONTENTS

Glimpses of Grace in the Old Testament

Encounters with Grace in the New Testament

Glimpses of Grace in the Old Testament

ABRAHAM

❧

Following God in a
Stop-and-Start Kind of Way

*P*eople often think that the God of the Old Testament is a God of wrath and vengeance; and at first glance, that might seem to be true.

His righteous character is certainly on display in the lives and events we find there.

But there are many other things about Him to be found in those age-old stories and the people who lived them.

Hebrews 11 describes these Old Testament saints as people who saw and welcomed God's promises "from a distance."

They only had glimpses of Who and what He was but those glimpses gave them the faith and strength to love Him and follow Him.

Over the coming weeks we will be looking at some of those Old Testament believers discovering what they saw "afar off" about God that transformed their lives.

These glimpses of God's grace have the potential to transform us too, if we are willing to learn from them and apply the truths to our own lives.

Today we'll look at what Abraham saw and what he shows us of God's faithfulness and undeserved kindness to us.

Abram, as he was called before God changed his name to Abraham, is a major figure in the Old Testament.

We first learn about him in Genesis 12, when God called him to leave his country, his people and also his "father's household" to go to a land that He would show him.

There, in that land, God promised to bless him and make him into a great nation, through whom all the families of the earth would be blessed.

Today we fully understand the meaning of that promise, because the Messiah, Jesus Christ, eventually came from Abraham's people and all people can have a relationship with God the Father, through faith in Jesus.

In John 8:56, Jesus said that Abraham, "saw My day and rejoiced."

So at some level, Abraham glimpsed that God's promise to him was extraordinary and eternal.

We don't know how God had made Himself known to Abraham before that call in Genesis 12. But Abraham obviously knew enough to listen and obey. Sort of.

Though God clearly told him to leave his family behind, Abraham initially took members of his family with him — his father and his orphaned nephew Lot.

They followed the river system from the city of Ur to Haran, probably to provide water for their flocks.

Though this was not the final destination God had in mind, Abraham and his family settled down in Haran, living there for five years until Abraham's father died.

We don't really know why he stopped there. Perhaps there were family issues.

Perhaps it was simply that it was a place of good pasture and of comfort, and they needed a break.

But I do think there is a warning for us here.

Because it is possible even for us to follow God in a stop-and-start kind of way, and when we get to a difficult place, or a comfortable place we become unwilling to risk anymore, so we stop moving forward with God.

But that kind of obedience isn't really the kind of obedience that brings the full blessing God wants for us.

When Abram moved on after his father's death, he still didn't fully comply with the call of God, because his nephew Lot stayed with him — a choice that would have some important consequences later.

Finally the group arrived in the place God had chosen for them.

The Lord appeared to Abram in Genesis 12:7-8 and announced that the land on which he now stood would be given to him and to his descendants forever.

He had finally arrived at the place of blessing!

And what did he do?

He built an altar to the east of Bethel and worshipped the God whose promise to him had been fulfilled.

Abraham knew this God was worthy to be followed and he knew He was worthy of worship.

There were a couple of problems, however. If you know the story, the land God gave Abraham wasn't empty ... it was filled with pagan, warring Canaanites!

Not only that, but it was experiencing famine and so perhaps, paying more attention to his circumstances than his God, Abraham kept on moving!

He let his fear of foes and famine drive him further south towards Egypt.

When he arrived in Egypt, he kept on making decisions based on his fears!

He imagined that Pharaoh would kill him in order to take his beautiful wife Sarah for himself; so Abram lied, claiming she was his sister – a deception that ended up with Sarah being taken from him anyway, right into the Pharaoh's harem!

We are not specifically told that Pharaoh slept with Abraham's wife, but we are not told that he didn't either.

But let me just reiterate that none of this had been God's idea!

In His mercy, God clearly intervened, revealed the lie and moved the ruler to quickly send them away with all their possessions and with their flocks!

It was surely only by God's grace that they survived!

They quickly returned to Bethel and the altar there, back where God's word had been confirmed to them and where the promise of blessing was.

To this point, Abraham hadn't necessarily followed the Lord perfectly, had he?

There were times he only partly obeyed, putting his own comfort or his own ideas above God's expressed command.

He stopped in Haran when he should have kept going and then he kept going to Egypt when he should have stopped in Canaan.

At times he based his decisions on fear rather than on faith and yet by the time he returned to Bethel, he had seen enough of God's grace to know that this God he was trying to follow would keep His Word, in spite of his own stumbles.

I think we can see that in the very next decision Abram had to make.

Lot was still with him and it was becoming evident that the situation could not continue.

Genesis 13 tells us that;

> [6] *the land could not support them while they stayed together, for their possessions were so great, So Abraham decided to separate from his nephew.*

In doing that, he did something quite remarkable...

As the older of the two, Abram had first choice of the land, yet he allowed Lot to take the best pasture around the "exceedingly wicked and sinful" towns of Sodom and Gomorrah while he chose the more arid land towards Jerusalem.

Do you see how Abraham was beginning to walk by faith and not by sight, trusting the God who had been faithful to him and making the deliberate choice to take God's path instead of his own?

Lot gladly went the way that looked easier but aligning himself with Sodom cost him greatly in the end!

We know that Lot initially prospered in Sodom as people often do, but it was not to last.

Several local kings banded together against the people of Sodom and Gomorrah plundering both cities and taking Lot and all his possessions captive.

One of Lot's servants managed to escape and quickly alerted Abraham to his relative's plight.

Despite the fact that Abraham could muster only 318 men to go with him, he put his trust in God and rode out against these kings and their vast armies freeing Lot, with all his people and possessions.

As Abram returned home from the defeat of the kings, he passed through a place known as the King's Valley where he met a mysterious individual by the name of Melchizedek.

Melchizedek brought out bread and wine and blessed Abraham in the name of God and Abraham responded by offering Melchizedek a tithe of everything he had.

This was an act of worship on Abraham's part and a recognition that God, whom Melchizedek served, was the source of all he possessed.

He knew where his blessings came from. He knew where his trust and fidelity belonged.

The King of Sodom also met him in that valley and he tried to "bless" Abraham as well by offering him all the goods he had recovered.

Custom would have allowed Abraham to keep some of the bounty; but doing so would have potentially aligned him with the King of Sodom and allowed the King to say he had made Abraham great.

Abraham refused to give God's glory to another.

He rejected the king's offer, though doing so put Abraham in a vulnerable position, and immediately after this God confirmed His promise to Abraham in one of the most important chapters in the Old Testament.

> *In Genesis 15 God first tells him: "Do not be afraid, Abram. I am your shield, your very great reward."*

God promised to be with him, to protect him and reward him!

He would be everything Abraham would need.

To confirm His Word, God entered into a solemn and unbreakable covenant with him promising the now 90-yr-old Abraham that he himself would father a child, an heir, who would have descendants too numerous to count!

> *And Genesis 15:6 tells us that Abraham "… believed the Lord, and … it (was) credited to him as righteousness."*

Though Abraham understood God's promise of a son and many descendants was unshakeable he didn't know how that would happen or exactly when!

So he and Sarah tried to help God out by conceiving a child with their servant girl Hagar!

Many of us wonder why Sarah might have willingly initiated such a thing?

In that culture there was such shame attached to the inability to bear children it was common custom for a wife to offer her maidservant to her husband to bear a child for him on her behalf.

But this decision to follow the culture rather than wait for God brought a lot of strife to Abraham's family strife that has lasted generations since!

Which unfortunately goes to prove that though we might be forgiven for our poor choices sometimes we don't get to choose the consequences for our actions.

After many more years of waiting, Abraham and Sarah, as they became known, did have a child of their own, a boy by the name of Isaac, whose name meant "laughter."

Abraham's faith journey with God certainly had its ups and downs.

He didn't always make the best choices…

And he didn't always learn from the mistakes he had made in the past!

At times it seems he struggled to trust the Lord.

But he was learning at every step that God's promises depended on God's faithfulness, not on his own understanding.

If we flash forward several years, to when Isaac was a young man, we see that God tested Abraham's hard-won faith as it had never been tested before.

I want to spend time in this story in Genesis 22 because it sums up all that Abraham had glimpsed of God in his long journey and it has so much to say to us today.

God appeared to Abraham one day and said, [2] *"Take your son, your only son, whom you love—Isaac—and go to the region of Moriah. Sacrifice him there as a burnt offering on a mountain I will show you."*

Can you imagine how difficult it was for Abraham to hear that?

It seems unbelievable doesn't it?

That God who is entirely good, would ask him to do something like that!

Isaac was to die at Abraham's own hand.

He was to be a burnt offering to the Lord – one in which nothing was held back from God as a symbol of complete dedication.

It is significant that Abraham was told to go to the Mount of Moriah because that mountain would become the site of the future Temple in which the people of Israel would worship God.

What was Abraham's response?

³ Early the next morning Abraham got up and loaded his donkey. He took with him two of his servants and his son Isaac. When he had cut enough wood for the burnt offering, he set out for the place God had told him about. ⁴ On the third day Abraham looked up and saw the place in the distance. ⁵ He said to his servants, "Stay here with the donkey while I and the boy go over there. We will worship and then we will come back to you."

Abraham did not tarry! He did not hesitate, but quickly set out just as God had commanded him.

I think it's worth noting though that he informed the servants in verse 5 that he and his son would go to "worship and then we will come back to you."

According to Abraham, both he and Isaac would return – and this is after God clearly told him that Isaac was to die!

⁶ Abraham took the wood for the burnt offering and placed it on his son Isaac, and he himself carried the fire and the knife. As the two of them went on together, ⁷ Isaac spoke up and said to his father Abraham, "Father?"

"Yes, my son?" Abraham replied.

"The fire and wood are here," Isaac said, "but where is the lamb for the burnt offering?"

⁸ Abraham answered, "God himself will provide the lamb for the burnt offering, my son." And the two of them went on together.

⁹ When they reached the place God had told him about, Abraham built an altar there and arranged the wood on it. He bound his son Isaac and laid him on the altar, on top of the wood. ¹⁰ Then he reached out his hand and took the knife to slay his son.

Isaac carried the wood on his back up the hill and though they had no animal, Abraham very clearly promises his son "God himself will provide the lamb for the burnt offering".

I know some have thought in the past that he was just being a good father, trying to protect his son from the terrible truth that he was about to die, but that is not what the Scripture tells us!

Hebrews 11:19 reveals that: ¹⁹ Abraham reasoned that God could even raise the dead, and so in a manner of speaking he did receive Isaac back from death.

Abraham thoroughly believed that his descendants would come through Isaac the son of promise.

Because Isaac had no children yet, Abraham reasoned that either his son would not die at all or God would raise him from the dead!

Either way, God's promise would be kept!

So what happened as Abraham raised the knife? Genesis 22:11 …

¹¹ But the angel of the Lord called out to him from heaven, "Abraham! Abraham!"

"Here I am," he replied.

¹² "Do not lay a hand on the boy," he said. "Do not do anything to him. Now I know that you fear God, because you have not withheld from me your son, your only son."

¹³ Abraham looked up and there in a thicket, he saw a ram caught by its horns. He went over and took the ram and sacrificed it as a burnt offering instead of his son. ¹⁴ So Abraham called that place The Lord Will Provide. And to this day it is said, "On the mountain of the Lord it will be provided."

God Himself did indeed provide a substitute to die in Isaac's place!

The one marked for death was set free by the death of another and Abraham called that place "The-Lord-Will-Pro-vide" because God did just that and Abraham and Isaac both returned to the other young men, just as Abraham said they would!

This is what it means that Abraham believed God and it was credited to him as righteousness!

He fully entrusted himself, his dreams and his hopes for the future to the One in whom he had believed!

I am sure you have already guessed that this whole event was a foreshadowing of Christ and all that He would one day come to do in that very same place.

Like Isaac, Jesus would ascend that very same hill with the wood of the cross on His back.

Jesus is the substitute sacrifice that the ram pointed to that day.

Michele Telfer

You see, God has done the very thing he asked Abraham to do!

God has offered His only Son the One whom He loved that we might know Him and be with Him.

John 3:16 is one of the most well-known verses in the world, but its' truth is for every one of us.

Listen to the love and promise it contains and put your name in there instead of "the world":

> *For God so loved the world that he gave his one and only Son, that whoever believes in him shall not perish but have eternal life. (John 3:16)*

We began today by referencing what Hebrews 11:13, says about the heroes of the faith like Abraham:

> *[13] All these people were still living by faith when they died. They did not receive the things promised; they only saw them and welcomed them from a distance. And they admitted that they were aliens and strangers on earth.*

Abraham saw the fulfillment of God's promises from afar.

Without fully understanding, Abraham believed that God is the God who gives life to those who trust in Him.

He believed that God would provide a sacrifice to die in our place.

In essence, he looked forward in faith to the same cross that we of the New Testament have the privilege of looking back upon.

What then, can we learn from the Glimpse of God's Grace that Abraham saw in the distance?

We can learn that God keeps His Word to us even when we stumble that when we choose Him over the world He blesses us. And that He Himself provides salvation to all those who believe and trust in Him!

May we, like Abraham, believe these things and trust Him completely!

Reflection and Discussion

Abraham didn't always look like the hero of the faith we see mentioned in Hebrews 11. For much of his life, he seemed to follow God in a stop-and-start kind of way — lingering in Haran for five years when he should've moved on and then allowing his fear of foes and famine to drive him to Egypt when he should've trusted God and stayed in Bethel. His poor decisions sometimes got him into trouble; and yet God continued to refine Abraham, bringing him to the point of being able to trust Him completely.

Ask God to speak to you. If possible, read the texts of Genesis 12:1-18:15; Genesis 21:1-7 and Genesis 22:1-14.

- God did not give up on Abraham or withdraw His promise from him despite his somewhat inconsistent journey. Do you fear you have made some missteps in your walk with the Lord? Are there places you have lingered when you shouldn't have? Are there relationships and even good, natural things that have held you back from what you know God has specifically told you to do?

- His faithfulness doesn't free us to follow Him half-heartedly, however. Jesus said we need to think about how we follow Him. Read what He told the multitudes gathering around Him in Luke 14:25-33. What is necessary for us to be His disciples?

- Between the hostile Canaanite inhabitants and the drought, Abraham must have started wondering if he'd heard things right! Would God be able to keep him in the place He'd called him to? Fear entered the picture. And once we start listening to fear, things can quickly get out of hand. What effects did Abraham's decision to lie to Pharaoh have on Sarah? On Pharaoh? On Abraham himself?

We really aren't operating well when we operate out of fear — whether it's fear of other people, fear of circumstances, or fear of the future. Everything gets out of balance and isn't seen clearly through the fog of worry and anxiety. The command "Fear not" is the most frequent command in the New Testament because God knows we are frail human creatures and He doesn't want us to be afraid. I Peter 5:7 urges us to, "Cast all your anxiety on Him because He cares for you." How about you? Is your life shaped by fear? Do you allow it to govern your decisions and your direction? Take a moment to think through what you are afraid of and cast those anxieties on Him. Talk to the Lord about each one. Ask for His help and then leave them with Him.

- It takes great faith to allow God to direct your path and choose for you. Lot chose what looked good — Abraham trusted God to choose what was best. Lot chose the promise of worldly success and prosperity — Abraham trusted God to choose what would come to him. Read what God said to Abraham in Gene-

Michele Telfer

sis 13:14-17. What speaks to your heart about His promise?

- Did anything surprise you about the story in Genesis 22 of Abraham's willingness to sacrifice Isaac?

- Abraham struggled with fear and made some truly poor decisions because of it. But looking through to the end of his story, we see that the missteps and stumbles became fewer and farther between. None of them prevented God from keeping His word to Abraham — from giving him the land and giving him a son. None of them stopped God from calling Abraham His friend! How does that encourage you?

Spend time in prayer thanking God for sending His one and only Son, Jesus Christ, to die as a sacrifice on your behalf. Ask Him to help you live worthy of the calling you have received for Christ's glory alone!

JOSHUA

Remembering God's Faithfulness in the Past

As we continue in our series on the Glimpses of God's Grace in the Old Testament we will be looking at the life of Joshua.

Many of us are familiar with Joshua as the one who bravely fought Israel's enemies and led them into the Promised Land but Joshua didn't become that great champion overnight. He went through some preparation in his life.

Joshua first enters the pages of Scripture in Exodus 17.

Israel had just crossed the Red Sea a few weeks before — not as an organized army, but as a band of former slaves newly released from 400 years of servitude in Egypt.

They were hardly prepared to face an enemy straightaway.

And though there were plenty of other older, more experienced men to choose from, Moses turned to Joshua to lead this first encounter with the inhabitants of the land a battle against the cruel nomadic tribe of Amalek at a place in the wilderness called Rephidim.

Verse 8...

> [8] *The Amalekites came and attacked the Israelites at Rephidim.* [9] *Moses said to Joshua, "Choose some of our men and go out to fight the Amalekites. Tomorrow I will stand on top of the hill with the staff of God in my hands."*

> [10] *So Joshua fought the Amalekites as Moses had ordered, and Moses, Aaron and Hur went to the top of the hill.* [11] *As long as Moses held up his hands, the Israelites were winning, but whenever he lowered his hands, the Amalekites were winning.* [12] *When Moses' hands grew tired, they took a stone and put it under him and he sat on it. Aaron and Hur held his hands up—one on one side, one on the other—so that his hands remained steady till sunset.* [13] *So Joshua overcame the Amalekite army with the sword.*

Most commentators believe Joshua was around 20 years of age at this time; and though young, he would have already seen much of God's power and Moses' leadership at work.

He would have been born a slave in Egypt.

He would have experienced that first Passover and crossed the Red Sea as they followed the pillar of fire and cloud.

He would have witnessed Moses strike the rock and would have drunk the water that miraculously sprang from it.

He would have seen manna fall from the sky and eaten his fill along with all the rest of Israel and so Joshua already knew from personal experience that the God they were following was the mighty God who saves and that Moses was His chosen leader.

So when Moses called him to lead the battle, Joshua didn't hesitate or question.

He responded in faith and obedience based on what he already knew of God's power and faithfulness.

Nothing gives us the impression that the men of Israel had any fighting ability at this time, but as Joshua stepped out in faith, he received a glimpse of God's grace that would mark a turning point in his life, preparing him for the future.

The amazing victory at Rephidim taught Joshua that it is the Lord who saves and that He will be with us in the battles of life.

But it also taught him how those battles are won.

Moses stood on the top of the hill and raised his staff while the battle was raging.

This was the staff that had parted the Red Sea and brought water from the rock in the desert.

Moses was calling down the power and presence of God on Joshua as he battled.

What encouragement Joshua must have received, looking up and seeing Moses praying for him, reminding him where the victory would come from!

I want you to notice as well that Moses didn't stand there alone. He needed the support of others to accomplish his part in what had to be done.

As fatigue slowly crept through Moses' arms Aaron and Hur partnered with him to steady his hands.

And I think that there's an important take-away in that for us as God has graciously placed us in community with others to help in our times of need – no one in His Kingdom should think of themselves as a lone ranger!

For just as Joshua needed Moses, so too Moses needed Aaron and Hur.

In the New Testament Paul reveals in 1 Corinthians 12 that as the children of God, we are like the members of Christ's body on earth.

We are one body, united in Him; but just like our biological bodies, the body of Christ has many individual parts.

Each of us is unique and necessary; and we have an important part to play as we work together to see God's purposes accomplished.

That day at Rephidim:

Joshua learned that God would never leave him or forsake him and that he was able to do all things through the One who gave him strength.

He learned how prayer changes things – making the impossible, suddenly possible.

And he learned the value of each one playing their part.

And though Joshua didn't realize it yet, God was going to use this event to equip him for the future that He had planned.

Immediately after their victory at Rephidim, God made a promise in Exodus 17:14 that He wanted Joshua particularly to hear:

> *¹⁴ Then the Lord said to Moses, "Write this on a scroll as something to be remembered and make sure that Joshua hears it, because I will completely blot out the name of Amalek from under heaven."*
>
> *¹⁵ Moses built an altar and called it The Lord is my Banner. ¹⁶ He said, "Because hands were lifted up against the throne of the Lord, the Lord will be at war against the Amalekites from generation to generation."*

A banner is something that identifies and unifies a particular group of people.

The Israelites' saying, "The Lord is my Banner," was a way of identifying themselves as the followers of the Living God who had promised to utterly defeat their enemies.

The same is true for us today. The Lord is our Banner in that He is the One who unites us. He is our Savior – we are rescued and set apart because of our faith in Him.

But what was it that God wanted Joshua to be sure to hear?

It was that He would "completely blot out the name of Amalek from under heaven."

This promise about the annihilation of the Amalekites prepared Joshua for what lay ahead.

Sometime later, Numbers 13 reveals that when God brought His people to the very edge of the Promised Land and they were poised to enter, He instructed that one man from each of the twelve tribes of Israel be sent ahead to spy out the situation and report back to Moses on what the land was like and whether the different tribes who lived there were "strong or weak, few or many."

After 40 days, the spies returned with two conflicting reports.

They brought with them huge clusters of grapes, as well as pomegranates and figs as proof of the land's goodness declaring that it was indeed a place of abundance that, in their words: "flowed with milk and honey."

And yet, ten of the spies were hesitant about Israel's ability to conquer the people living there, saying they felt like grasshoppers when compared to them! Apparently, there were some actual physical giants in the land!

Only two of the spies, Joshua and Caleb, disagreed with that assessment.

They believed that God would help them no matter who their adversaries were.

Why do you think Joshua in particular would feel so confident about their chances against the people who lived in the land God had promised them?

Well, Scripture reveals that one of the groups living there was in fact the Amalekites, whom God had promised to completely wipe out.

Remember that God specifically wanted Joshua to know that He was going to remove the Amalekites from the equation and not allow them to hinder His people any longer.

Joshua remembered both God's promise and His past faithfulness and applied it to the situation they were now in!

If God could defeat the Amalekites, He could surely defeat all the other "ites" in the land as well, even the "giants" that so terrified the other spies.

It was faith in the promise of God and the sure knowledge of His faithfulness in the past that fueled Joshua and Caleb's obedience.

They weren't "just being positive." They weren't just being brave.

They were acting in utter faith that God would do exactly as He said He would and bring His people into the land so Joshua encouraged them to "take possession of the land" believing that in God's strength they could certainly do it!

Unfortunately, the rest of Israel were unwilling to trust the Lord.

They were reluctant to follow God into the land He had sworn to give them and so they were sent to wander in the wilderness for 40 long years — one year for each day they'd spent spying out the land.

With the exception of Joshua and Caleb, that entire generation of men who had come out of Egypt died in the wilderness.

They were not allowed to enter God's Promised Land because of their unbelief.

This story so touches my heart because I realize that as I face my own problems today, my own "giants" in the land, I have to ask myself whether I'm viewing my problems through eyes of fear, or eyes of faith?

Am I looking to God and His faithfulness or to my own abilities? Am I trying to do things on my own or do I call on my brothers and sisters in Christ's family to pray for me and receive their help and encouragement?

The truth is: we do not face our struggles alone!

Even in the midst of life's fiercest battles – God has promised to never leave us nor forsake us as we trust in Him.

After the 40 years of wandering, Moses himself died. Israel was once again poised to enter the Promised Land…but this time without their deliverer and leader.

We often forget how large Moses loomed in the life of Israel.

He was the only leader most of them had ever known. He was the voice of God in their midst, the one who taught them everything they knew about the Lord. And now, when they most needed him, he was gone.

God appeared to Joshua and appointed him as leader of His people to take them in to the land He had sworn to give them.

He understood that Joshua must have been reeling with sorrow and fear, so He gave him a series of solemn promises and instructions in Joshua 1:6-7 and 9

> *⁶ Be strong and courageous, because you will lead these people to inherit the land I swore to their ancestors to give them.*

⁷ "Be strong and very courageous. Be careful to obey all the law my servant Moses gave you; do not turn from it to the right or to the left, that you may be successful wherever you go ... ⁹ Have I not commanded you? Be strong and courageous. Do not be afraid; do not be discouraged, for the Lord your God will be with you wherever you go."

What promises! What strength Joshua must have found in them to go forward in obedience!

It was not long before Joshua found himself in a situation that would certainly prove the truth of God's promises.

In Joshua 3, Israel once again was on the border with the Promised Land. They were camped just east of the Jordan River, directly across from the walled city of Jericho.

They were exactly where God had led them. They believed God's promise to be with them as He had been with Moses and to take them into the land.

But they hadn't necessarily anticipated facing a river swollen to twice its normal width or a walled fortress on the horizon!

Turn with me to Joshua 3:2 where we find Joshua's instructions to the people ...

² After three days the officers went throughout the camp,³ giving orders to the people: "When you see the ark of the covenant of the Lord your God, and the Levitical priests carrying it, you are to move out from your positions and follow it. ⁴ Then you will know which way to go, since you have never been this way before. But keep a distance of about two thousand cubits between you and the ark; do not go near it."

Faced with an unexpected challenge, they didn't look for an alternative plan or move from where God had placed them. They simply waited.

They were waiting for the Ark of the Covenant to lead them.

The Ark of the Covenant was the symbol of the presence of God.

The Ark was always kept in the midst of the congregation, either in the Holy of Holies when Israel was encamped or in the center of the marching arrangement when Israel was on the move.

But here, God revealed that the Ark was to go in front of the congregation, showing the Israelites where to go.

God knew they hadn't experienced anything like this before, and He wanted them to have a clear sign that He was with them, leading them and keeping them safe.

God's care for us is so particular and so tender. At all times, He knows exactly where we are, what we are facing, and He knows exactly what we need but we must be careful not to rush ahead of Him as I think we sometimes do asking Him to BLESS what we've already decided to do, without ever waiting for His direction before we begin!

We want HIM TO FOLLOW US rather than the other way around and then we wonder why things often do not turn out as we had hoped!

But if we wait for Him, He will go before us to show the way and, as we obey His Word to us, He will remain with us — even in a flood of many waters!

Look at Joshua 3:14-17. What happened when the priests' feet got wet and the Ark entered the river?

> *¹⁴ So when the people broke camp to cross the Jordan, the priests carrying the ark of the covenant went ahead of them. ¹⁵ Now the Jordan is at flood stage all during harvest. Yet as soon as the priests who carried the ark reached the Jordan and their feet touched the water's edge, ¹⁶ the water from upstream stopped flowing. It piled up in a heap a great distance away, at a town called Adam in the vicinity of Zarethan, while the water flowing down to the Sea of the Arabah (that is, the Dead Sea) was completely cut off. So the people crossed over opposite Jericho. ¹⁷ The priests who carried the ark of the covenant of the Lord stopped in the middle of the Jordan and stood on dry ground, while all Israel passed by until the whole nation had completed the crossing on dry ground.*

What an incredible glimpse of God's grace!

Just as He had been with Joshua in the face of seemingly insurmountable odds at Rephidim the Lord was with them now as they faced the impossible challenge of crossing a swollen river.

As the priests stepped into the rushing water it began to slow and as the Ark stopped in the middle of the Jordan, the people completed the crossing on dry ground!

How wonderful, how miraculous!

And yet the real glimpse of God's grace was that Ark standing firm on dry ground in the midst of the river because it proved that God was right there in the middle of their trial with them, ensuring their ultimate safety!

And just as He met them in the midst of their difficulties – He will also meet us in the midst of ours to bring us to safety!

I marvel at the fact that the priests had to step out into the swiftly moving water before the river began to subside!

That was a very different scenario to how God's people had crossed the Red Sea under the leadership of Moses.

Then the Sea had dried up before they ever took a step, but that was not the case this time!

And I think it goes to remind us of the vital role faith will play as we follow God.

He may not lead us in just the same way He has led someone else – or even in the way He led us previously.

Each person's walk with God may look different from ours; and each season of our own lives presents different challenges, yet we can trust Him in all of them.

Joshua 4:1 reveals that this encounter with God at the Jordan river was something He meant for them to remember always…

> *¹ When the whole nation had finished crossing the Jordan, the Lord said to Joshua, ² "Choose twelve men from among the people, one from each tribe, ³ and tell them to take up twelve stones from the middle of*

the Jordan, from right where the priests are standing, and carry them over with you and put them down at the place where you stay tonight."

[4] So Joshua called together the twelve men he had appointed from the Israelites, one from each tribe, [5] and said to them, "Go over before the ark of the Lord your God into the middle of the Jordan. Each of you is to take up a stone on his shoulder, according to the number of the tribes of the Israelites, [6] to serve as a sign among you. In the future, when your children ask you, 'What do these stones mean?' [7] tell them that the flow of the Jordan was cut off before the ark of the covenant of the Lord. When it crossed the Jordan, the waters of the Jordan were cut off. These stones are to be a memorial to the people of Israel forever."

Isn't it amazing that these stones – the building blocks of their testimony, if you will – came from the middle of the river!

Israel needed these stones. They would help them keep the story of God's deliverance alive for their children and their children's children.

Unfortunately, the people of Israel had exhibited very short memories to this point!

They often forgot all that God had done for them in the past and they repeatedly struggled with unbelief. They needed help remembering.

Are we really any different? I don't believe we are.

When we feel His presence and His power in the midst of trials, we must pay careful attention for these are our memorial stones — the markers in our lives that demonstrate His mercy, His grace and His love for us.

And they will be immensely useful to us in the future.

There are many incidents in the Bible in which individuals are called to look back on their own "memorial stones" of God's faithfulness in the past in order to give them courage and hope for the future. The Psalms are full of such encouragements.

As I have faced my own difficulties in life I have found that practice of remembering to be most helpful to me too!

There have been many times that God has taken me by a route that I would never have chosen for myself.

Some of the incidents that spring to my mind would be the terrible pregnancy I had with my first child.

It seemed certain that we would lose him, but God graciously protected both his life and mine in the end and though I was advised not to have more children, God in His kindness gave me a daughter as well.

Our family moved across the world, from Africa to the United States – a land we did not know — and yet God miraculously provided for every step of that journey.

Years later I had another near-death experience.

I was critically ill; and when I was admitted into the hospital, the doctor with two nurses as witnesses took down my end-of-life decisions in case I did not make it.

But God reminded me of His faithfulness to me in the past and encouraged me from the words of Psalm 139 that despite the doctor's assessment, all of my days were written in

God's book before one of them came to be and that I would live just as long as He had always planned.

The fact that I'm here today is another memorial stone of testimony in my pile!

All of these testimonies of God's grace in the past helped me a few years ago when my husband died and I found myself alone after 35 years of marriage… for though there have been many times that God has taken me by a route that I would not have chosen for myself. I can tell you that God has met me and walked along side me through each trial and yes, He is faithful in all things!

And I know that He will graciously meet you too as you remain obedient to His Word and as you trust in Him!

There was another reason given for these memorial stones in Joshua 4 though.

They served as a public witness to the nations that God is the mighty God who saves.

When we share our testimony with someone, we are doing just that — we are declaring Him to those around us.

But if we're honest, most of us struggle with what to say and how to say it, don't we?

Don't make it more difficult than it really is. You don't have to tell your whole story all at once.

Little by little, in the normal course of your relationships and activities, ask God to give you opportunities to just mention Him and His grace…humbly and lovingly because we never really know what is in someone else's heart.

Let Him open the doors. And when you do that, you will find the words will come and they will accomplish His purpose.

What did Joshua glimpse of God's grace and what can we see in his life about the God we too want to follow?

We see that our God is a God who keeps His promises in the face of battles, loss and unexpected challenges.

He strengthens and guides us through His Word.

He remains faithful from generation to generation.

And He never leaves us or forsakes us. Never.

What grace! May we glimpse it for ourselves and give our lives completely to the One who loves us far more than we can ever imagine.

Reflection and Discussion

Joshua was able to act in faith because of what he had come to know about God. He saw that God keeps His promises. He saw that the Lord remains faithful from generation to generation in the face of battles, loss and unexpected challenges. He will never leave us or forsake us and He promises to stand with His people in their time of need if they will but trust His Word and follow Him. God longs for us to see the same glimpses of His grace too!

- Ask God to speak to you as you read the texts of Exodus 17:8-16; Joshua 1:6,7 & 9; and Joshua 3:2—4:7.

- What stood out to you about the story of the battle at Rephidim? How do you suppose Joshua was affected by seeing Moses praying on the hill for him? What do you think Joshua took away from the experience?

- We saw that Aaron and Hur came alongside Moses to help him as he prayed for Joshua in the battle. Moses knew he couldn't do what needed to be done by himself. How would you describe your relationships with others in the body of Christ? Do you keep them at arm's length, preferring to do things on your own? Are you cooperating with them? Learning from them?

Serving them as they serve Christ? What do you sense the Holy Spirit would have you change in this?

- Though Joshua didn't realize it at the time, facing the enemy here at Rephidim actually prepared him for things he would later encounter, as we saw in Joshua 1 and Joshua 3. Can you think of a circumstance you faced or a decision you made that turned out to prepare you for something further down the road?

- When Israel first approached the border of the Promised Land, Joshua was sent out with 11 others to spy out the land and report back to Moses. When they returned, ten of them could only focus on the giants that were there. They lost sight of the greatness of their God. Only Joshua and Caleb saw things clearly. And only Joshua and Caleb were allowed to enter the Promised Land. The other 10, and indeed that whole generation died in the wilderness because of their unbelief. Think about a problem you are facing right now. How are you looking at it — with eyes of fear or eyes of faith? Are you placing your confidence in your own abilities or in the promises of God? How can you begin to exercise faith in this situation?

- It must've been hard for Joshua to lose his mentor Moses and yet it was then that he received his own call from the Lord. God told him to have courage as He promised to be with him. He also called him to value and carefully follow His Word. Think of a time that God met you in a challenge you didn't anticipate or feel prepared for. How did the promise of His presence and the truth of His Word encourage you?

- When faced with the flooding river what stood out to you about their willingness to wait for God's direction? How quickly do you tend to make decisions? Do you seek God first or do you tend to just ask Him to bless what you've already decided to do? Do you need to change anything in the way that you face obstacles?

- Of course, the flooding river wasn't the last difficulty that Joshua and his people faced as they entered and settled the Promised Land. Think of a time in your life when you set out to obey God and things got really hard. What did you do? Did you begin to doubt His Word? Did you try to help Him out by coming up with alternatives to His clear direction? What did you learn from the experience? How can you begin to use these experiences as memorial stones in your life?

Spend some time in prayer asking God to increase your faith in His promises, to open your eyes to His leadership in your life and to show you those you need to come alongside of in His work. And then ask Him to remind you of His faithfulness to you in the past so that the remembrance of His grace will give you hope and strength for the future.

RAHAB

No One is Too Far for God to Reach

*I*n our last lesson as we learned of the glimpses of God's grace in the life of Joshua, we discovered that when God brought His people to the edge of the Promised Land the first time, their focus had been more upon their own deficiencies than on God's power and the certainty of His promises.

Believing themselves to be small, weak and ineffective – like grasshoppers when compared to their adversaries they turned away in unbelief from the land that God had given them and were forced to wander in the desert for 40 years.

During those nomadic years, they successfully faced many opponents.

The outcomes of those battles, coupled with what had happened to Pharaoh's army at the Red Sea when they fled Egypt, meant that the Israelites' reputation preceded them.

Or perhaps more accurately, the reputation of their God preceded them causing fear in the hearts of those they had yet to encounter!

Today we focus on God's amazing grace shown to one of their adversaries, as we go back in time to just before Israel crossed over the Jordan River.

The well-fortified city of Jericho loomed on the horizon, just five miles from the river. It stood guard over the fords of the Jordan.

This Canaanite city was built on a mound for defensive advantage and seemed totally impenetrable because of its high, thick walls.

Following Moses' example all those years before, Joshua chose to send out spies on a reconnaissance mission to assess Jericho's real strength.

I think that he had learned from his own mission all those years before though, because he secretly sent out only two men.

Once within the city walls, the spies met the subject of our study today – a woman by the name of Rahab.

Turn with me to Joshua 2:1 …

> *¹ Then Joshua son of Nun secretly sent two spies from Shittim (where they were encamped). "Go, look over the land," he said, "especially Jericho." So they went and entered the house of a prostitute named Rahab and stayed there.*

It may seem strange to us that the spies, who essentially were on a "holy mission", would immediately seek out a prostitute but I think it makes good strategic sense after all, who would be able to tell you what the fighting men were talking about, if not the woman who was supplying them with wine and entertainment!!

It was not long, however, before someone reported the Israelites' presence in the city to the King of Jericho.

Learning they were with Rahab, the king quickly commanded the prostitute to: "Bring out the men who came to you and entered your house, because they have come to spy out the whole land."

Verse 4 …

> *⁴ But the woman had taken the two men and hidden them. She said, "Yes, the men came to me, but I did not know where they had come from. ⁵ At dusk, when it was time to close the city gate, they left. I don't know which way they went. Go after them quickly. You may catch up with them."*
>
> *⁶ (But she had taken them up to the roof and hidden them under the stalks of flax she had laid out on the roof.) ⁷ So the men set out in pursuit of the spies on the road that leads to the fords of the Jordan, and as soon as the pursuers had gone out, the gate was shut.*

Rahab does the extraordinary — she puts her own life in danger by not only hiding the spies, but by lying to the ruler!

In those days, the gates of walled cities were shut at night for protection and Rahab, professing ignorance, claims that the men slipped out of the city as night was falling.

Though she insists that she did not know where the spies were going, it would not be difficult for the king to guess they might be headed in the direction of the fords.

Without a doubt Rahab showed remarkable courage that day, but why did Rahab do what she did?

Why did she hide them and lie to protect them?

The answer is found in what she says to the spies in verse 8-11:

> *8 Before the spies lay down for the night, she went up on the roof 9 and said to them, "I know that the Lord has given you this land and that a great fear of you has fallen on us, so that all who live in this country are melting in fear because of you. 10 We have heard how the Lord dried up the water of the Red Sea for you when you came out of Egypt, and what you did to Sihon and Og, the two kings of the Amorites east of the Jordan, whom you completely destroyed. 11 When we heard of it, our hearts melted in fear and everyone's courage failed because of you, for the Lord your God is God in heaven above and on the earth below.*

This is so interesting! Her report of how her people viewed the Israelites is exactly what God had promised Moses years before!

In Exodus 23:27 the Lord had sworn:

> *27 "I will send my terror ahead of you and throw into confusion every nation you encounter. I will make all your enemies turn their backs and run." and again in Deuteronomy 2:25 God affirmed: 25 This very day I will begin to put the terror and fear of you on all the nations under heaven. They will hear reports of you and will tremble and be in anguish because of you."*

Can you imagine how often stories of the Israelites and their God had been repeated in Jericho over the past 40 years?

First there would surely have been reports of the parting of the Red Sea and the destruction of Pharaoh's army.

Then came the accounts of how the Israelites followed a pillar of cloud by day and a pillar of fire by night and how these signs were something to do with the power and presence of their God.

More recently there was the destruction of the Amorite Kings.

These stories had been circulating over the years and Rahab of all people, would have heard the rumors from the men who came through her doors!

If their hearts melted in fear it was because people were talking about the Israelites and their God who went before them!

I often think in pictures! Can you imagine the scene in Jericho as the Israelites approached?

Suddenly one night someone looks out of their window in the wall and says: "What is that strange glow to the east?"

In the morning, an unusual cloud formation seems to have settled the other side of the Jordan River and the people of Jericho suddenly realize that this nation they'd heard about and the God who accompanied them had arrived!

Can you imagine what it must've been like in that city?

They must've been terrified!

Their only consolation was that the Jordan River was between them and this group massing on their border and thankfully, that river was in full flood at the time!

Believing themselves to be safe — at least until the river subsided — all of Jericho held their breath.

However, the very message that caused the hearts of her countrymen to melt in fear caused Rahab's heart to believe God.

It was by the grace of God that Rahab had come to this point.

For not only was He working to His plan, preparing the way for His people to inhabit the land. He had also been preparing Rahab to receive the message of His deliverance.

Only God can prepare a human heart to believe in Him.

Only God can order circumstances and awaken understanding to create that moment when someone begins to believe.

And believe she does, because in verse 11 she calls Him not only Lord of heaven above, but Lord of the earth below as well!

She pleads with the spies in verse 12 …

> [12] *"Now then, please swear to me by the Lord that you will show kindness to my family, because I have shown kindness to you. Give me a sure sign*[13] *that you will spare the lives of my father and mother, my brothers and sisters, and all who belong to them—and that you will save us from death."*

Rahab asked for deliverance for herself and for her family.

And I think she shows us it is not enough to just be acquainted with God, we must be willing to cast our lot in with Him and become part of His people.

This is an important truth for us all to grasp.

It is not just enough to know about God — even James warns in the New Testament in James 2:19 "You believe that there is one God. Good! Even the demons believe that—and shudder."

According to John 17:3 eternal life is that we know the One true God and Jesus Christ whom He has sent and the word "know" in that verse speaks of knowing by experience, not just by hearing.

It is so much more than head knowledge. In fact, the word was often used to speak of the intimate relationship of a husband and wife.

It is a deeply personal experience of the life of another person. That is what God desires us to have with Him.

And I think this has become a real issue for us in the world of today.

Many of us have Bibles and studies and internet messages at our fingertips. Knowledge about God is available everywhere, yet, unfortunately, it seems to have resulted more in apathy than in reverence and obedience, as was Rahab's experience!

It's very easy today to "settle" on the edges of faith where not much is required but life is good and can go on as usual.

Rahab didn't have that luxury. Her decision that day was quite literally a matter of life and death and really, it still is.

The spies responded …

> *14 "Our lives for your lives!" the men assured her. "If you don't tell what we are doing, we will treat you kindly and faithfully when the Lord gives us the land."*
>
> *15 So she let them down by a rope through the window, for the house she lived in was part of the city wall. 16 She said to them, "Go to the hills so the pursuers will not find you. Hide yourselves there three days until they return, and then go on your way."*

We are told that Rahab actually lived in the wall of the city.

Recent archaeological excavation at the Old Testament site has produced findings that are absolutely consistent with the Biblical account.

It seems Jericho had two walls.

The outer wall was 12 feet thick, the inner wall 6 feet thick and there is evidence that as the city became more crowded, people had made their homes in the fifteen-foot gap between the two.

Remarkable isn't it that Rahab's home was in the very wall that fell!

Likely Rahab and the spies had no idea of the real danger she would be in, living within the wall itself but God prompted the spies to give her specific instructions before they disappeared into the night.

Verse 17 …

17 Now the men had said to her, "This oath you made us swear will not be binding on us 18 unless, when we enter the land, you have tied this scarlet cord in the window through which you let us down, and unless you have brought your father and mother, your brothers and all your family into your house. 19 If any of them go outside your house into the street, their blood will be on their own heads; we will not be responsible. As for those who are in the house with you, their blood will be on our head if a hand is laid on them. 20 But if you tell what we are doing, we will be released from the oath you made us swear."

I find this so touching and affirming.

They probably hadn't expected to encounter a pagan woman who wanted to know their God!

How do you explain faith as you're escaping for your lives through a window?

They shared what they knew.

They knew God had saved them from death in Egypt by the scarlet blood of the lamb on their doorposts.

By faith, they offered her that same message of deliverance, trusting that God would honor His name and her faith.

And what is that message we see in the Passover and in the scarlet cord in Rahab's window?

It is that Salvation is by faith in the shed blood of Christ for "without the shedding of blood there is no forgiveness" Hebrews 9:22 and while Christ's blood is available for everyone, only those who shelter under it are delivered.

During the Passover, the Israelites had to stay in their homes while the death angel passed over, or be lost themselves; and in just the same way, Rahab and her family had to remain in her house until God moved against Jericho or the promise would not be of any effect.

Rahab for her part, obeyed.

She didn't drape the cord on a shelf and look over at it from time to time.

She didn't lay it aside, planning to hang it at the last minute.

She put it in the window just as she was told.

Faith is not what we say or what we think — it is what we do!

It is not mental agreement with a set of facts. It is casting yourself on those facts, trusting them to be true and living by them.

That is why Hebrews 11:1 uses words like "substance" and "evidence" to describe faith.

Faith isn't just something we feel or think — it is a conviction that can (and must) be demonstrated.

21 "Agreed," she replied. "Let it be as you say."

So she sent them away, and they departed. And she tied the scarlet cord in the window.

²² When they left, they went into the hills and stayed there three days, until the pursuers had searched all along the road and returned without finding them. ²³ Then the two men started back. They went down out of the hills, forded the river and came to Joshua son of Nun and told him everything that had happened to them. ²⁴ They said to Joshua, "The Lord has surely given the whole land into our hands; all the people are melting in fear because of us."

Joshua 2 ends with Rahab waiting in her house — obedient to the message the spies had delivered and trusting in the scarlet cord to mark her for deliverance.

Meanwhile, the spies returned to the camp with their report; and then things began to happen.

As we saw in Joshua 3 and 4, the Israelites miraculously and very publicly crossed the Jordan River on dry ground, throwing even more fear into the hearts of the already terrified inhabitants of Jericho.

They set up camp at Gilgal and made the twelve stones into a memorial.

And under the watchful eye of their enemies the first thing they did was celebrate the Passover.

Decades before, the first Passover had started their journey to the Promised Land and now another Passover was about to end it!

As they ate food from the Promised Land for the first time, the manna ceased just as God said it would.

God was establishing the spiritual life of His people to begin a new chapter in their journey.

Meanwhile Rahab waited and trusted.

When everything was ready in the nation of Israel, God moved against their enemies.

Joshua 6:1 …

Now the gates of Jericho were securely barred because of the Israelites. No one went out and no one came in.

> *² Then the Lord said to Joshua, "See, I have delivered Jericho into your hands, along with its king and its fighting men. ³ March around the city once with all the armed men. Do this for six days.⁴ Have seven priests carry trumpets of rams' horns in front of the ark. On the seventh day, march around the city seven times, with the priests blowing the trumpets. ⁵ When you hear them sound a long blast on the trumpets, have the whole army give a loud shout; then the wall of the city will collapse and the army will go up, everyone straight in."*

We're familiar with the story.

Can you imagine how that scene might have played out over the first six days? How the fear within the city would have been growing day by day?

And when the marching strategy changed on day seven, I'm sure the people crowded onto the wall, straining to see what that meant.

Can you imagine the noise and the reverberations that surrounded them?

When the military march in rhythm it is known as cadence, what you may not know is that when a fighting force come to a structure such as a bridge they can never march in cadence while crossing it.

They have to break rhythm because the cadence of their march would actually cause the bridge to collapse!

Did God use something like the extra weight and the marching and the noise to destabilize the wall as part of the miracle?

We don't know!

The only thing we do know from both the Scripture and the archaeological evidence is that the wall did fall!

Interestingly, a German excavation of the wall that took place from 1907-1909 discovered that there was a small section of the northern wall around Jericho that did not fall which gives rise to the question: is that where Rahab's house stood?

What do you think?

Whatever the case, once the wall fell Rahab's wait was over! Her faith was vindicated!

Judgment came on everything and everyone in Jericho — but that judgment passed over Rahab and her family because they were sheltered under the scarlet cord.

Joshua ordered the two men who had spied out the land in verse 22...

²² ... "Go into the prostitute's house and bring her out and all who belong to her, in accordance with your oath to her." ²³ So the young men who had done the spying went in and brought out Rahab, her father and mother, her brothers and sisters and all who belonged to her. They brought out her entire family and put them in a place outside the camp of Israel.

²⁴ Then they burned the whole city and everything in it, but they put the silver and gold and the articles of bronze and iron into the treasury of the Lord's house.

There is something else very important to see here: Rahab was delivered because she persevered in her faith. She kept on believing, kept on trusting to the end.

Nearly three weeks had passed since the spies had left her house. There were days when she saw and heard nothing that would indicate the promise was coming.

Then came the days when she saw God beginning to move as the Israelites marched silently around the city.

I cannot help but wonder what would have happened if she had given up and removed the scarlet cord before that seventh day?

But her faithfulness eventually had an effect on her whole family's future.

Although Rahab and her family were initially placed outside the Israelite's camp that's not where she was left!

We are told in verse 25 that…

25 ... Joshua spared Rahab the prostitute, with her family and all who belonged to her, because she hid the men Joshua had sent as spies to Jericho—and she lives among the Israelites to this day.

Because of God's incredible grace, Rahab was welcomed into the nation of Israel and dwelled with them.

She was included in His people. What a future and what a hope that gave her!

Think of everything that would have worked against this ever happening for her.

Her people were enemies of God. She was a pagan, probably an idol-worshipper. She was a woman. And what's more, she'd been a prostitute. Not someone you'd welcome to your feast, right?

However, the grace goes beyond even that because we learn in Matthew 1:5 that Rahab is listed in the human lineage of Jesus Christ, the Messiah.

She married a man named Salmon, who was a leader in Israel.

In fact, tradition tells us he was one of the two spies who rescued her!

She became the mother of Boaz, and from there the line continues through David and ultimately to Mary, the mother of Christ.

Rahab is one of only four women besides Mary mentioned in the genealogy of Christ — something very unusual in Jewish genealogies altogether — and interestingly each of the four has some taint or scandal you would not expect to see in a royal line.

Two were even from foreign nations!

But God is no respecter of persons. He doesn't play favorites. And His plan has always included people from every nation, every group, every background.

What an incredible God we serve!

God's grace is just the same today …

It doesn't matter where we've come from or what we've done.

Nothing can disqualify us from salvation except unbelief.

Romans 3:23 reveals that "all (of us) have sinned and fall short of the glory of God." Like Rahab, we desperately need to be reconciled to Him.

Rahab turned away from her people and from the culture of the day to trust the God whose grace she glimpsed from afar and in doing so, she received the full, complete salvation He offers.

God longs to include us in His family just as He did Rahab — we need only believe in Him — and shelter under the scarlet cord of Christ's blood that He has provided!

Reflection and Discussion

Rahab's story proves that it doesn't matter where we've come from or what we've done. Nothing disqualifies us from salvation except unbelief.

Ask God to speak to you as you read the texts of Joshua 2:1-24 and Joshua 6:1-25.

- What stood out to you about the initial encounter between Rahab and the spies — and more especially, what she said to them?

- The very message that caused the hearts of her countrymen to melt in fear caused her heart to believe God. She may not have known everything that was going on; but she knew enough. And what is that "enough"? Look at Hebrews 11:6 — what does real faith look like?

- We don't often think about it, but we all operate from certain assumptions or basic truths. Hebrews tells us that there are basic truths underlying everything: There is a God who rules both heaven and earth and He wants to relate to you in love. Think about your own life for a moment. Would you say your life is based on these truths? How do your choices, your relationships, your goals reflect that belief?

- Rahab was able to find God even while living in the culture she did. How hard do you think it is to find God? Do you think of Him as being far-off and remote, sitting behind a cloud somewhere waiting for you to figure things out?

- In the lesson we talked about the parallels between the spies' instructions and the Passover Feast they were soon to celebrate in the Promised Land. What do you remember about their similarities?

- Rahab was told to hang the scarlet cord from her window. She didn't drape the cord on a shelf and look over at it from time to time. She didn't lay it aside, planning to hang it at the last minute. She put it in the window as she was told. Faith is not what we say or what we think — it is what we do. It is not mental agreement with a set of facts. It is casting yourself on those facts, trusting them to be true and living by them. Do you think we do this today?

- Our situation as believers today is much like Rahab's. She was looking for deliverance from the coming destruction of her city. What are we looking for according to Titus 2:13?

- There is something else very important to see here: Rahab was delivered because she persevered in her faith. She kept on believing, kept on trusting to the end. When the disciples came to Jesus in Matthew 24 with questions about the end of all things, He described the upheavals, the lawlessness and the lack of faith that would characterize the world before His return. What sobering words did He give them in verse 13?

- Rahab is listed in the human lineage of Jesus Christ, the Messiah. His plan has always included people from every nation, every group, every background. How does that encourage you?

Spend some time in prayer thanking God for His grace and for the fact that in Christ He has removed our sins from us as far as the east is from the west!

ELIJAH

A Person Just Like Us

*J*oshua had been the leader of God's people when they crossed into the Promised Land, but after he died the nation was not as consistent about following God as they should've been.

They began to drift; and during the period known as the time of the Judges Israel entered an era where "… every man did what was right in his own eyes".

Throughout this time the same pattern was repeated again and again.

The children of Israel would slide into worshiping the "gods of the people who were all around them"

And so the Lord would then deliver them "into the hands of their enemies" causing the Israelites to eventually cry out to the Lord again as their only hope!

In response, God would raise up a deliverer, a Judge who would lead them in the ways of the Lord but their obedience was always short lived, and as soon as the Judge died they would forget about God and go off to do worse than they had done before.

This ongoing cycle was repeated until the Prophet Samuel, who was the last of God's Judges.

It was then that the people, in a desperate attempt to be like the other nations around them, demanded their own king.

The rule of earthly Kings however led to increasing disunity and division with the people moving further and further from the God who loved them.

As we begin our study today we pick up the story at what was arguably one of the lowest times in the history of God's people when King Ahab ruled the northern territory.

He and his wife Jezebel have become almost synonymous with wickedness and treachery.

Ahab married the pagan Jezebel for political reasons. She was from Sidon, a neighboring kingdom known for its worship of Baal.

And she had been quick to introduce Baal worship into everyday life for the people of the Northern Kingdom.

Baal was one of the most horrible deities ever devised by human imagination.

His name meant "master" or "owner"; and he was thought to control all the forces of life and nature.

Everything was supposed to be subject to him. And he was a cruel god who demanded all sorts of abominations from his followers.

For example, if a person wanted Baal's blessing on their home, they were required to bury their own child alive in the foundation of the house to please this false god!

Ahab and Jezebel openly worshipped Baal and actively supported all the prophets who followed him. Because of that worship of the true and living God was all but eradicated from the everyday life of His people.

It was at this dark time that God raised up one of the most important people in the Old Testament and certainly one of the most memorable — the prophet Elijah. Only Moses has a greater position of honor among the prophets.

Let's read from 1 Kings 17:1 …

> *Now Elijah the Tishbite, from Tishbe in Gilead, said to Ahab, "As the Lord, the God of Israel, lives, whom I serve, there will be neither dew nor rain in the next few years except at my word."*

Elijah is described simply as "the Tishbite" — in many ways, a man from nowhere, a person of no particular significance.

I take great encouragement from that because God not only knows how to raise up leaders when they are most needed very evidently, He can use anyone — even a person from nowhere — to do His will as He did with Elijah!

Elijah identifies himself as servant of the true God of Israel and essentially issues a direct challenge to Ahab: "My God lives — yours does not. My God is in control — yours is not."

Elijah pulled no punches. He boldly declared himself to be on God's side.

There's something else we need to note here. Elijah was not confronting the king in his own name or in his own strength.

And Elijah's message wasn't his own. It was based on a warning God had given years before.

The Lord had cautioned His people through Moses in Deuteronomy 11:16-17 to:

> [16] *Be careful, or you will be enticed to turn away and worship other gods and bow down to them.* [17] *Then the Lord's anger will burn against you, and he will shut up the heavens so that it will not rain and the ground will yield no produce, and you will soon perish from the good land the Lord is giving you.*

Though Elijah's words were definitely a challenge to Ahab and his false god, they were also a call to Israel to remember their God, to return to Him and worship Him alone.

Elijah longed for Israel to return to God.

After Elijah delivered the Lord's message to the King, God directed him to a brook in the Kerith Ravine east of the Jordan River where the prophet would be safe from the rage and persecution his pronouncement would surely provoke.

We don't have time to look at it, but you may be familiar with the story. Elijah stayed at the brook for a while, drinking its water and being fed with the food brought to him by ravens.

Certainly God wanted to keep Elijah safe from the repercussions of his original message to Ahab and Jezebel. But He was also wanting to teach Elijah some lessons.

There were some things he could only learn in a hidden place — things like dependence and trust. Things he would need for the battle he was soon to face.

With the ongoing drought, the brook eventually dried up; but Elijah did not move until the Word of the Lord came to him once more this time directing him into Jezebel's home territory of Sidon, where God had prepared a widow to take care of him.

Verse 8…

> *8 Then the word of the Lord came to him: 9 "Go at once to Zarephath in the region of Sidon and stay there. I have directed a widow there to supply you with food." 10 So he went to Zarephath. When he came to the town gate, a widow was there gathering sticks. He called to her and asked, "Would you bring me a little water in a jar so I may have a drink?" 11 As she was going to get it, he called, "And bring me, please, a piece of bread."*
>
> *12 "As surely as the Lord your God lives," she replied, "I don't have any bread—only a handful of flour in a jar and a little olive oil in a jug. I am gathering a few sticks to take home and make a meal for myself and my son, that we may eat it—and die."*
>
> *13 Elijah said to her, "Don't be afraid. Go home and do as you have said. But first make a small loaf of bread for me from what you have and bring it to me, and then make something for yourself and your son.*
>
> *14 For this is what the Lord, the God of Israel, says: 'The jar of flour will not be used up and the jug of oil will*

not run dry until the day the Lord sends rain on the land.'"

I am quite sure that Elijah must've wondered why God would use a widow of all people to provide for him …

But I do think that God calls us to live daily in His grace.

We, like Elijah, are to trust that He will provide exactly what we need when we need it.

We often don't want to be totally dependent on God; but the reality is that we can only learn to trust by having to trust.

We can only learn daily dependence by having things come a day at a time. And those lessons need to go deep into our hearts and lives.

Elijah spent two years with the widow before the Word of the Lord came to him again, telling him to appear before Ahab with another message.

God was going to keep His Word.

But something important had to happen before He could act, ending the drought and sending the rains one again: Baal and his prophets had to be proven totally false and impotent.

They could never be allowed to claim credit for what God alone was going to do.

When Elijah met with Ahab in 1 Kings 18 he immediately challenged the King and his prophets of Baal and Asherah to meet him on Mount Carmel. People from all over Israel were also to attend.

I'm sure Ahab probably expected some sort of ceremony at which Elijah would announce the end of the drought.

Michele Telfer

He couldn't have envisioned what was really going to happen.

In 1 Kings 18:21 Elijah began by posing a question to the gathered crowd: "*How long will you waver between two opinions? If the Lord is God, follow him; but if Baal is God, follow him.*" But the people said nothing.

Perhaps the people feared to answer because Ahab was there.

Perhaps they honestly didn't believe in their God anymore.

Perhaps the years of faithlessness had totally sapped their ability to take a stand.

Regardless, their silence was a sad response to the faithfulness God had always shown them.

Elijah quickly laid down the rules for a contest that would prove just who the living God was.

Ensuring that the odds were heavily stacked against him from the beginning, he allowed the prophets of Baal every advantage in their choice of bull, declaring that they could slaughter the better offering and arrange it just as they pleased.

He would take whatever was left.

Then Elijah encouraged the false prophets to: "call on the name of (their) gods" saying that he would call on the name of the Lord "and the God who answers by fire, He is God."

The false prophets eagerly agreed; however, no matter what they did and no matter how much they called, no fire fell from heaven.

Even when Elijah mocked them encouraging them to shout louder in case Baal was meditating, or sleeping and needed to be awakened, they were helpless — no one answered them and no one paid attention!

When the time of the evening sacrifice to God arrived, Elijah finally stepped forward to make his offering.

He drenched the sacrifice, the wood and the rocks of his altar with jar after jar of precious water. And then Elijah began to pray.

> *"Lord, the God of Abraham, Isaac and Israel, let it be known today that you are God in Israel and that I am your servant and have done all these things at your command. 37 Answer me, Lord, answer me, so these people will know that you, Lord, are God, and that you are turning their hearts back again.*
>
> *38 Then the fire of the Lord fell and burned up the sacrifice, the wood, the stones and the soil, and also licked up the water in the trench.*
>
> *39 When all the people saw this, they fell prostrate and cried, "The Lord—he is God! The Lord—he is God!"*

God answered Elijah's brief prayer in a very clear and powerful way.

Fire fell, consuming not only the sacrifice but the wood, the water, the stones and even the dirt under the altar. Nothing was left.

There was no question God had answered the prayers of His prophet.

As the people turned to the Lord in worship, Elijah had the prophets of Baal executed — and lest you feel sorry for them, remember the many child sacrifices they encouraged.

But even then, Elijah knew the work was not over.

He needed to ask God to send the rain. So while Ahab left for Jezreel, Elijah went to pray.

He prayed intensely, repeatedly sending his servant to look for clouds on the horizon.

Seven times he prayed, until at last, one small cloud appeared.

And when the rains finally came, the downpour was so great that many scholars believe that Ahab's chariot may have become stuck in the thick mud of the valley allowing Elijah to outrun Ahab's chariot and be the first one back in Jezreel!

No one seems to know exactly why Elijah rushed to Jezreel.

Perhaps he was anticipating a great revival would break out in the city and that the king and queen would be deposed.

Perhaps he wanted to make sure Ahab didn't take the credit for what God had done.

Regardless, there he was — the most wanted man in Israel — back within the reach of those he had just defeated.

This whole event is an incredible glimpse of the grace of God!

He answers the prayers of His people and it encourages me to really assess the requests I make of God.

Are they rooted in His Word or in my own desires?

And am I willing to persevere in faith, waiting expectantly for Him to answer as Elijah did?

I Kings 19:1-4 reveals what happened next:

> *¹Ahab told Jezebel everything Elijah had done and how he had killed all the prophets with the sword. ² So Jezebel sent a messenger to Elijah to say, "May the gods deal with me, be it ever so severely, if by this time tomorrow I do not make your life like that of one of them."*

> *³ Elijah was afraid and ran for his life. When he came to Beersheba in Judah, he left his servant there, ⁴ while he himself went a day's journey into the wilderness. He came to a broom bush, sat down under it and prayed that he might die. "I have had enough, Lord," he said. "Take my life; I am no better than my ancestors."*

Every battle has its aftermath; and when Elijah receives the death threat from the enraged Jezebel, his heart gives way to fear and he runs for his life.

This passage of Scripture has always had a powerful effect on me.

Elijah had the faith to believe God would keep His Word and deal with His people as He said He would.

He had the faith to believe God would answer with fire to consume the sacrifice.

He had the faith to believe God would send rain despite the initial absence of clouds.

But here, he ran in fear and was overcome by what can only be described as depression.

And I think it's important for us to understand that even those who are mightily used of God can struggle at times with feelings of fear or failure.

But it's also important for us to realize that fatigue and physical needs can affect the way we react to stressors and that it is wise to address those needs first.

Physical exhaustion certainly played a part in Elijah's response.

He was in desperate need of sleep, food and drink; and God miraculously gave him all of those things.

At the brook Kerith, God used ravens to bring him food.

At Zarephath, God used a poor widow to sustain him for two years.

But here in the wilderness under a dying broom bush, God sent angels to give his prophet exactly what he needed to go on.

What a glimpse of God's grace to us, that He knows our human weaknesses and doesn't despise us for them.

Instead, He graciously and kindly provides for us.

But beyond physical rest and recuperation, Elijah had a spiritual need.

He needed to hear from God about the disappointment he was bearing. Why hadn't Israel turned completely to Him? Why were Ahab and Jezebel still in power?

So he did what he had learned to do: he went to a place where he could hear from God.

Strengthened by the nourishment God Himself provided, he went to Mt. Horeb, where God had appeared to Moses.

I love God's tender care of His hurting prophet.

At Israel's lowest point, Elijah had spoken for God. And now, at Elijah's lowest point, God speaks to him.

God begins by asking Elijah a simple question: "What are you doing here, Elijah?"

Can I point out that God is omniscient – He knows everything!

He already knows why Elijah has come and yet He asks the question to engage Elijah and to get him thinking.

For his part, Elijah is very honest with the Lord.

He reminds God of his passionate service emphasizing …

"I have been very zealous for the Lord God Almighty. The Israelites have rejected your covenant, torn down your altars, and put your prophets to death with the sword. I am the only one left, and now they are trying to kill me too."

In many ways, I think that Elijah was looking for "success" — for some indication that his work had not been in vain.

In other words, he was disappointed in the results. He'd expected more. He wanted more.

Elijah felt like a failure and Elijah felt totally alone!

But neither of those two assessments were actually correct, as we shall soon see.

Many prophets of the Old Testament felt just like Elijah. They were ignored, scorned, mocked, even killed for speaking God's word.

But the success of the prophet is not ever measured by whether or not the people respond to their message.

No, the success of a prophet is only really measured by whether or not they did what God told them to do!

The same is true for you and me.

So how does God address the fault in Elijah's thinking? Let's pick up the story in verse 11 …

> *11 The Lord said, "Go out and stand on the mountain in the presence of the Lord, for the Lord is about to pass by."*

Then a great and powerful wind tore the mountains apart and shattered the rocks before the Lord, but the Lord was not in the wind. After the wind there was an earthquake, but the Lord was not in the earthquake. *12 After the earthquake came a fire, but the Lord was not in the fire. And after the fire came a gentle whisper.*

When God speaks to Elijah His voice is not in the mighty wind, nor in the earthquake, nor in the raging fire, but rather His voice comes to His servant in a gentle whisper — proving that God doesn't always work in the way we would expect.

He moves in ways we don't always understand. He moves in ways we cannot control.

Sometimes He works dramatically, breaking stones and sending wind and fire.

Sometimes He whispers so that we have to almost strain to hear.

But He is always at work — even in what we perceive to be silence.

What a glimpse of His grace we can cling to in our own struggles. He is there and He will speak if we can quiet ourselves to hear.

God repeats His question to Elijah: "Elijah, what are you doing here?" And Elijah repeats his complaint to the Lord, word for word. But then the Lord gently begins to refocus Elijah's attention.

Verse 15-18 …

> *15 The Lord said to him, "Go back the way you came, and go to the Desert of Damascus. When you get there, anoint Hazael king over Aram. 16 Also, anoint Jehu son of Nimshi king over Israel, and anoint Elisha son of Shaphat from Abel Meholah to succeed you as prophet. 17 Jehu will put to death any who escape the sword of Hazael, and Elisha will put to death any who escape the sword of Jehu. 18 Yet I reserve seven thousand in Israel—all whose knees have not bowed down to Baal and whose mouths have not kissed him."*

God reminded Elijah he was not alone — indeed he never had been serving alone.

God had reserved 7,000 in Israel besides Elijah who had not followed Baal.

Then God turned Elijah's eyes to the future, to the kings waiting to be anointed and to the young man, Elisha, who would succeed him as prophet.

Far from rebuking Elijah for his self-pity and complaining, God simply turned his attention to the work still awaiting him.

He was not finished with his prophet after all.

I think we can take great encouragement from the glimpses of grace we have seen in Elijah's life.

The first glimpse would be that God hears our prayers and answers them.

James confirms in the New Testament in James 5:16 that:

> *"The prayer of a righteous person is powerful and effective."*

But sometimes we have the mistaken idea that people in the Bible are super-saints — that they have "super-faith powers" that enable them to live unaffected by the same things we have to face.

But Elijah is our proof that is not so and James immediately follows his statement about the effectiveness of prayer declaring in the following verses that:

> *"¹⁷ Elijah was a man, just like us. He prayed earnestly that it would not rain, and it did not rain on the land for three and a half years. ¹⁸ Again he prayed, and the heavens gave rain, and the earth produced its crops."*

Elijah was certainly a human being with strengths and weaknesses.

But he was also a righteous man — one who had placed his faith and trust in God for the forgiveness of sin.

We saw salvation pictured in the life of Rahab last week.

But if you are still wavering, still trying to decide if you can commit to Him, now might be the perfect time to simply admit your need of a Savior and place your trust in the shed blood of Christ that has paid the price for your sin.

Just ask God to forgive you and to give you His righteousness.

The second glimpse of God's grace in the life of Elijah is how He supplies all our needs.

He took care of His prophet at Kerith, at Zarephath and in the wilderness. In different ways at different times, but He always supplied what was needed and just as He met with Elijah in his disappointments He will meet us in ours.

If you find yourself fully committed to serving the Lord and yet like Elijah you're feeling a bit burned-out and disappointed in your lack of "success" if you're wondering why the blessings haven't come yet and you're struggling, first pay attention to any physical needs you may have.

Do you need some rest, some food, are you dehydrated?

But then, as did Elijah, intentionally get yourself into a place where you can hear from the Lord.

Remember, you can talk honestly with Him about your disappointments and your desires to serve Him, so pray.

Pray honestly. Pray intently.

But don't forget to also be quiet and listen for His voice. He will speak.

Then look ahead with hope to the future and follow Him more closely than ever before. He will never leave you or forsake you.

Reflection and Discussion

*J*ames 5:17 tells us that Elijah was a human being with strengths and weaknesses just like us. But James is using Elijah's life to remind us that the prayers of a righteous person are both powerful and effective — human weakness notwithstanding!

Elijah shows us that God hears His people — those who have been made righteous by trusting in Him for salvation — and He is faithful to supply our needs in every circumstance.

Read 1 Kings 17—19 and ask God to speak to you. Be sure to listen for His small still voice.

- What impresses you about Elijah's first encounter with Ahab in 17:1? How was the God he served different from the gods Ahab and Jezebel followed?

- We've seen how the Word of the Lord repeatedly came to Elijah. Can you think of how God has spoken to your heart recently? Did it come through the Scriptures, through the words of a friend or in some other way? How did you know it was the Lord speaking?

- At both the brook and at the widow's home in Zarephath, God taught Elijah to truly depend on Him for his day-to-day provision. How would that dependence help Elijah in the battles that lay ahead of him? How has the Lord helped you learn to trust Him?

- What stood out to you about Elijah's encounter with the prophets of Baal and his own prayer for rain on Mount Carmel?

- After all of God's faithfulness to him, why do you suppose Elijah was so distressed at Jezebel's threats?

- God did not meet Elijah in the desert in the cataclysmic way we might expect, but rather through the gentle whisper of His voice. What do you think God wanted Elijah to learn from that?

- When God did not fully meet his expectations, Elijah was deeply shaken; and, coupled with physical exhaustion, he fell into a very dark place emotionally. He felt like a failure and he felt alone; but neither of those two assessments turned out to be true. Has something caused you to feel like a failure in your service for the Lord? What do you think the Lord would have you do, based on Elijah's example?

- Think of a struggle you are facing right now. Is it possible your perceptions of the situation are not quite right? Ask the Lord to help you discern what is really true. What is God saying to your heart? What do you think He wants you to do about it?

- God did not berate Elijah for the way he was feeling. Instead, He met his needs, both physical and spiritual. Are you as compassionate to those around you who might be struggling?

- After considering how Elijah prayed, how would you like your prayer life to be different?

Spend time in prayer asking God to speak to you, remembering that He is still at work even in the perceived silences — perhaps we just need to listen more closely.

JEHOSHAPHAT

When We Don't Know What to Do

*I*n this lesson we study the life of Jehoshaphat, son of Asa. He ruled the Southern Kingdom of Judah at the same time the wicked Ahab and Jezebel ruled the Northern Kingdom of Israel.

Jehoshaphat was very aware of what was going on in Israel; and the first thing he did was strengthen his borders against the growing evil he saw in the North.

But that wasn't the only way in which he showed wisdom. Scripture reveals in 2 Chronicles 17:3-4 that…

> *³ The Lord was with Jehoshaphat because he followed the ways of his father David before him. He did not consult the Baals ⁴ but sought the God of his father and followed his commands rather than the practices of Israel.*

Jehoshaphat was proving to be as good a king as Ahab was a bad one!

He followed the example of his ancestor King David — not the example of Israel.

He sought God and followed Him — not the "baals" or false gods all around him.

The "baals" referred to here aren't just the one Baal we learned about last week. There were hundreds of these false gods or "masters" throughout the land.

Generally, they were worshipped in "high places", which were literally sites up on the mountains where anyone could go to worship whatever false deity they chose.

And I think it's not really any different today — because in a way people still want to worship a god of their own making, rather than the God who is!

Perhaps our "baals" aren't quite so easily recognized; but they are just as numerous, just as "appealing" and just as dangerous to true faith.

A modern idol might be an actual material object; but it might also be an idea or a philosophy or practice that falsely promises life and happiness.

An idol really is anything that captures our affections and draws us away from God.

Verse 6 tells us that Jehoshaphat's "heart was devoted to the ways of the Lord" and while he prepared his country militarily to face their opponents, he knew they needed to be prepared spiritually as well.

And he knew that could only happen as they understood and obeyed the Word of God.

Michele Telfer

So he removed the high places and the wooden images that were destroying the faith of his people.

And he sent priests and leaders across his kingdom to teach God's Word from town to town.

This was the most important thing he could ever have done. The book of Hebrews tells us God's Word changes us at the core of who we are.

As the people of Judah began to learn and obey God's Word, their relationship with the Lord was restored. But there was another effect as well.

Verse 10 tells us "The fear of the Lord fell on all the kingdoms of the lands surrounding Judah, so that they did not go to war against Jehoshaphat."

I believe this is the first glimpse of God's grace that we see in the life of Jehoshaphat — God honors those who honor His Word. The people of Judah prospered in every way when they obeyed Him.

The Scripture says Jehoshaphat himself was blessed with "riches and honor in abundance." It was a time of peace and prosperity in the land.

And then, quite surprisingly, Jehoshaphat allowed his son to marry the daughter of Ahab — the very king he was guarding his borders against!

It makes no sense, does it?

In reality, Jehoshaphat was disobeying the very Word of God he was teaching his people to obey.

God had consistently commanded His people not to intermarry with those who worshipped idols because He knew that would ultimately lead them into sin, grief and disaster.

It's hard to imagine what could have led Jehoshaphat to make such a dangerous compromise.

Did he grow careless and begin to think he could handle anything?

Had he been worn down by a lovesick son begging to marry the girl of his dreams?

Was he the victim of a conspiracy on the part of Ahab and Jezebel to weaken Judah and bring it under their control?

We can find many "reasons" for every unwise decision that is made.

Unfortunately, one unwise decision often leads to others and Jehoshaphat's inevitable "visit with the in-laws" resulted in that very thing.

King Ahab wanted to go to war against Syria.

What better way to cement the growing alliance between the two kingdoms than to go to battle together?

And what better opportunity for the cunning Ahab to possibly rid himself of the prosperous and faithful Jehoshaphat?

Amazingly, Jehoshaphat agreed to the proposition!

But he hadn't completely lost touch with the need to seek God and so he insisted that they seek the counsel of the Lord before they set out.

Ahab brought in 400 of his false prophets, but Jehoshaphat refused to seek wisdom from any of them.

He knew that a servant of the living God was needed; and ignoring Ahab's objections, he sent for a man of God by the name of Micaiah — a man Ahab hated because he never prophesied anything favorable to the king.

As could be expected, the false prophets all proclaimed exactly what they knew King Ahab wanted to hear.

They promised a great victory and encouraged him to go to war.

Though Michaiah was pressured to agree with their words, he refused to speak anything other than what the LORD gave him.

He mockingly repeated the advice of the false prophets as if he agreed with them; but Ahab recognized what he was doing.

And so he made Micaiah swear an oath to speak "nothing but the truth in the name of the Lord."

So he did. Micaiah boldly informed Ahab that the Lord planned disaster for him and promised the king, "If you ever return safely, the Lord has not spoken through me."

One can only wonder what must have been going through Jehoshaphat's mind as he saw all this drama played out before him?

Was he uncomfortable with all the lying and deceit of the false prophets?

Was he drawn to the truth he heard from God's prophet — or was he embarrassed by it?

Did he feel trapped and see no way out of the complicated situation he had created for himself?

We don't know, but we do know he went forward with the decision to go to war with Ahab.

I think we've all been there at one time or another caught in a situation that we didn't envision or one we thought we could avoid – and then making another bad decision to try to resolve it.

In looking back, we might even wonder, why didn't God stop me? Why didn't He put on the brakes and keep me from doing something that wasn't wise?

Well, in His grace, He often does. He arranges things so our plans don't work out, things fall through or we simply can't go forward.

He actually did that at other times in Jehoshaphat's life but here, God didn't intervene and though He revealed the truth of things through Micaiah, He didn't prevent Jehoshaphat from making his own poor decisions.

But I think that that, too, is the grace of God.

He doesn't treat us like pawns on a chessboard or slaves who have no will of their own.

He made us in His image. He has given us the ability and the freedom to choose.

He just longs for us to make the right choices.

Unfortunately, the decision to go to war was not the only poor decision Jehoshaphat made.

Let's continue reading in 2 Chronicles 18:28 …

> *28 So the king of Israel and Jehoshaphat king of Judah went up to Ramoth Gilead. 29 The king of Israel said to Jehoshaphat, "I will enter the battle in disguise, but you wear your royal robes." So the king of Israel disguised himself and went into battle.*

I honestly don't understand Jehoshaphat here when he agrees to go into battle as the only one who was clearly identifiable as a king!

Not surprisingly we learn in verse 30 that "the king of Israel" was the particular target of their opponent …

> *30 … the king of Aram had ordered his chariot commanders, "Do not fight with anyone, small or great, except the king of Israel." 31 When the chariot commanders saw Jehoshaphat, they thought, "This is the king of Israel." So they turned to attack him, but Jehoshaphat cried out, and the Lord helped him. God drew them away from him, 32 for when the chariot commanders saw that he was not the king of Israel, they stopped pursuing him.*

What grace God showed Jehoshaphat!

He was in trouble because of his own unwise choices; yet when he cried out, God heard and helped him.

The Syrian soldiers retreated and Jehoshaphat was saved.

I can't help but think Ahab must have felt totally protected in his armor even as he watched Jehoshaphat being chased down by the Syrian soldiers.

You can almost hear Ahab chuckling in his helmet at the brilliance of his whole scheme!

However, the battle was far from over, verse 32 …

> *33 But someone drew his bow at random and hit the king of Israel between the breastplate and the scale armor. The king told the chariot driver, "Wheel around and get me out of the fighting. I've been wounded." 34 All day long the battle raged, and the king of Israel propped himself up in his chariot facing the Arameans until evening. Then at sunset he died.*

It's worth noting that Jehoshaphat's life was saved even though he wore only robes, yet Ahab was killed despite his armor!

The text says an archer "drew his bow at random and hit the King of Israel" in the most vulnerable spot possible, but there was nothing random about it!

The prophet Elijah had earlier spoken the message from God that Ahab would one day be killed by the very King of Aram who was in the battle that day. Ahab was well aware that his days were numbered.

Perhaps that's why he went into battle in protective armor.

He was still trying to defy God. But despite Ahab's deceitful strategies, God kept His promise. His purpose was fulfilled.

This whole account just goes to prove that a person cannot outsmart or outmaneuver God.

The Lord knows how to guard His own and how to mark the unjust for punishment.

Though God protected him, Jehoshaphat's alliance with the ungodly Ahab could not simply be passed over. He needed to see what he had really done.

As he returned home, the Lord sent the prophet Jehu out to greet him with an unsympathetic message, revealed in 2 Chronicles 19:1-4. God's servant challenged the king asking:

"Should you help the wicked and love those who hate the Lord? Because of this, the wrath of the Lord is on you."

Those must have been hard words for Jehoshaphat to hear.

I don't imagine he had thought about his decisions in quite that way: "I am loving and helping wicked people who hate God by doing this."

But that is how God saw his actions.

Give him his due though, Jehoshaphat repented of what he had done and he immediately made an about-face.

He renewed his commitment to God. And then he did the same for his people. He brought them back to the Lord, the God of their fathers.

I love what this teaches us — that when we make wrong choices, God treats us as beloved children. He doesn't ignore our disobedience, He cares enough to rebuke us — to correct us — and to show us the truth of what we have done and He doesn't always remove the consequences of our actions, but He never leaves us to deal with them alone and He always shows us a way forward.

So what consequences did Jehoshaphat have to live with as a result of his wrong choices?

Remember that as his reign began, no one in the region had dared come against him; but the alliance he made with Ahab's northern kingdom had been interpreted as a sign of weakness by those around him, and now he was seen as vulnerable.

The result was that several armies moved against him.

2 Chronicles 20, proves however that he had learned from his recent experience with Ahab for as soon as he heard news of the approach of the three armies of "Ammon, Moab and Mount Seir" who had joined forces against him the alarmed Jehoshaphat knew what to do with his fear.

He immediately called the nation to a day of fasting in order to seek God without distraction.

Look at how the king prayed once his people were gathered in Jerusalem in verse 5 and 6 of that chapter:

> [5] *Then Jehoshaphat stood up in the assembly of Judah and Jerusalem at the temple of the Lord in the front of the new courtyard* [6] *and said: "Lord, the God of our ancestors, are you not the God who is in heaven? You rule over all the kingdoms of the nations. Power and might are in your hand, and no one can withstand you.*
>
> [7] *Our God, did you not drive out the inhabitants of this land before your people Israel and give it forever to the descendants of Abraham your friend?* [8] *They have lived in it and have built in it a sanctuary for your Name,*

saying, ⁹'If calamity comes upon us, whether the sword of judgment, or plague or famine, we will stand in your presence before this temple that bears your Name and will cry out to you in our distress, and you will hear us and save us.'

Jehoshaphat began by affirming God's supremacy over all the kingdoms and nations of the earth.

After witnessing what had happened to Ahab in the recent past he knew that "power and might" belonged to the Lord and he acknowledged that no one could withstand God.

He reminded the Lord of His promise to Abraham and affirmed that they were crying out to God as their only source of hope.

Jehoshaphat believed that God would hear and that He would save His people, just as He had done so many times before.

Recognizing that they could not face the vast army that stood against them in their own strength, Jehoshaphat asked the Lord to deal with their enemies, proclaiming: "(Lord) we do not know what to do, but our eyes are on you."

What an incredible prayer!

There have been many times that I have used these very words when facing a problem of my own Lord, I don't "know what to do, but (my) eyes are upon You." and just as He did with Jehoshaphat, God has answered me, showing me a way where there seemed to be no way.

As the whole nation stood before the Lord, the Holy Spirit came upon a priest there by the name of Jahaziel, who spoke a message of encouragement to the crowd in verse 15 …

> *15 He said: "Listen, King Jehoshaphat and all who live in Judah and Jerusalem! This is what the Lord says to you: 'Do not be afraid or discouraged because of this vast army. For the battle is not yours, but God's. 16 Tomorrow march down against them. They will be climbing up by the Pass of Ziz, and you will find them at the end of the gorge in the Desert of Jeruel. 17 You will not have to fight this battle. Take up your positions; stand firm and see the deliverance the Lord will give you, Judah and Jerusalem. Do not be afraid; do not be discouraged. Go out to face them tomorrow, and the Lord will be with you.'"*

This was an interesting word from the Lord, to say the least!

Jehoshaphat had thousands of soldiers at his disposal, superbly trained and probably itching for a fight.

But God said no. The battle was not theirs, but His. He would fight for them. They would not have to do a thing.

We are told in verse 18 that at this …

> *18 Jehoshaphat bowed down with his face to the ground, and all the people of Judah and Jerusalem fell down in worship before the Lord. 19 Then some Levites … stood up and praised the Lord, the God of Israel, with a very loud voice.*

Instead of questioning God's instructions or running to sharpen their swords or get their weapons together anyway, just

Michele Telfer

in case the people of Judah bowed down in worship of God and they began to praise Him by faith for what He was about to do!

I am challenged by this for I realize that instead of fretting in my own difficulties, I should be praising the God who goes with me.

And instead of wringing my hands in fear, perhaps I should be praising Him in advance of seeing Him act!

King Jehoshaphat and his people took the time to cry out to God and they worshipped and praised Him — focusing on His glory and His faithfulness rather than on their fear.

The next morning, they rose early and began their preparations to go out to face the armies of Ammon, Moab and Mount Seir, just as God had instructed.

But as they marched, the King and his officials placed singers out in front of the soldiers to sing praise to God for His mercy and grace.

The Scripture tell us in verse 22 that …

> [22] *As (Israel) began to sing and praise, the Lord set ambushes against the men of Ammon and Moab and Mount Seir who were invading Judah, and they were defeated.* [23] *The Ammonites and Moabites rose up against the men from Mount Seir to destroy and annihilate them. After they finished slaughtering the men from Seir, they helped to destroy one another.*

We are not told exactly how it happened — how these: "ambushes" were set by the Lord but somehow disagreement broke out between the different armies and those who had been allied against God's people only moments before suddenly turned on one another!

I can imagine each group boasting about how many of God's people they would kill in battle then arguing about whose boasts were better then proving their swordsmanship skills on each other!

We don't know exactly what happened but Scripture tells us that Ammon and Moab slaughtered the whole of the Edomite army from Mount Seir and then they turned on one another until not a man was left alive!

And when Jehoshaphat and his men got to an overlook where they could see the battlefield, it was just as God had promised.

He had completely and utterly destroyed the enemy.

All that remained was for the men of Judah to collect the plunder — which was so vast it took them three days to gather it together.

Then Scripture tells us...

> ²⁶ *On the fourth day they assembled in the Valley of Berakah, where they praised the Lord. This is why it is called the Valley of Berakah to this day.*
>
> ²⁷ *Then, led by Jehoshaphat, all the men of Judah and Jerusalem returned joyfully to Jerusalem, for the Lord had given them cause to rejoice over their enemies.* ²⁸ *They entered Jerusalem and went to the temple of the Lord with harps and lyres and trumpets.*
>
> ²⁹ *The fear of God came on all the surrounding kingdoms when they heard how the Lord had fought against the*

enemies of Israel. ³⁰ And the kingdom of Jehoshaphat was at peace, for his God had given him rest on every side.

They gathered in the Valley of Berachah, which means: the Valley of Blessing.

That speaks to me because though the enemy's attack may have certainly seemed like a low point — a valley of fear — in the life of the nation God had turned it into a valley of blessing for them instead.

And I love that they returned together to Jerusalem as well.

This was no chaotic, every-man-for-himself victory celebration as other armies might indulge in.

No, the men of Judah had come out as one; and they would return as one.

They had come out honoring God and focused on Him. They would return in the same manner.

So they went to the Temple, still singing and praising God.

The account ends with the words …

"³⁰ And the kingdom of Jehoshaphat was at peace, for his God had given him rest on every side. The nations around them feared the God who had fought for His people, and Jehoshaphat's kingdom enjoyed peace once again."

This is such a glimpse of God's grace and we would do well to apply it to our own lives — for He will also move against our enemies as we seek Him and focus on Him and His glory!

We face enemies today as well.

Paul reveals in Ephesians 6:12 that:

"our struggle is not against flesh and blood, but against the rulers, against the authorities, against the powers of this dark world and against the spiritual forces of evil in the heavenly realms."

For though those spiritual powers are already defeated by the death and resurrection of Christ, they are still trying to destroy the people God loves before their final end.

And we are to battle them in the same way Jehoshaphat did. Standing in God's power — in His spiritual armor and singing His praises!

We can see many glimpses of God's grace in the life of Jehoshaphat.

We see that God honors those who honor Him and His Word.

Jehoshaphat's heart was devoted to the Lord's ways, and God gave his kingdom rest and prosperity.

To this day, Jehoshaphat is remembered as one of the good kings in the history of God's people.

We also see that God loves us enough to correct us when we stumble and to lead us back to the right path.

When Jehoshaphat failed to trust in and obey the Lord, making poor decisions and leading his people astray, he was quick to respond to God's correction. And God forgave him and reestablished both him and his kingdom.

And we see that God goes before us as we come against our enemies.

When we go forward in faith, trusting His Word, following His instructions, seeking His glory above our own, He fights for us and gives us His peace.

Whatever you may be facing, I pray that Jehoshaphat's prayer on the eve of his battle will truly become yours: "Lord, I know not what to do, but my eyes are on You."

I know from my own experience that our faithful God will show you what you need to do. Trust Him.

Reflection and Discussion

*J*ehoshaphat is one of the good kings in Israel's history and yet he was not perfect. He made mistakes and occasionally wandered from God's path; but in times of distress Jehoshaphat cried out to the Lord and by His grace, God answered in the most remarkable ways.

Read 2 Chronicles 17:1-13; 2 Chronicles 18:1—19:2 and 2 Chronicles 20:1-30 asking God to speak to you.

- In Jehoshaphat's day people wanted to serve a God of their own making rather than the God who is. Do you think the same is true even today? How do you see that in our culture?

- An idol can be literally anything that captures our affections and draws us away from God. Can you think of some false things people might follow today?

- Jehoshaphat tore down the high places where the false gods were worshipped; and because he understood the transforming power of God's Word, he sent out priests and officials to teach it. How has God's Word affected your life? In what ways has it changed you?

- Unfortunately, Jehoshaphat disobeyed the very Word he was teaching his people to obey when he allowed his son to marry Ahab's daughter. What stood out to you about what happened as a result?

• It's hard to believe that even after God's prophet Micaiah warned of impending disaster, Jehoshaphat still went into battle with Ahab. Why do you think he persisted with that unwise decision?

• God does not see us as pawns on a chessboard. He allows us the freedom to choose Him and His way, or not. Why do you suppose He allows free will? How do you think Jehoshaphat's perception of God and the world changed as a result of what happened?

• Has there ever been a time in your life when God said "no" and stopped you going a certain way? How did you respond to that? In retrospect, did you come to see it as His protection?

• Ahab was unable to escape the judgment of God no matter how many schemes he carried out. Does that encourage you or frighten you? Why?

• God saved Jehoshaphat in the battle; and though he learned from his error, there were still consequences to be endured because of his initial choice — the neighboring rulers attacked him. How did Jehoshaphat respond to his enemies' threat? What are the principles that stood out to you from the story? Are there any consequences you are facing today from a poor decision in the past? How does Jehoshaphat's example help you?

• In every trial we should first pray. We should be willing to praise God in advance of seeing Him act. We should follow His commands (without making our own plan B). But more than that, we should "show up" — we should take our place. When you face difficulties, do you continue to do the work God has called you to? Do you continue to show up? Or do you rather lie on your bed waiting for Him to "fix things"?

- Israel's valley of fear ended in the Valley of Blessing. How has a valley in your own life been turned into a place of blessing by the Lord?

Think of a seemingly impossible situation in your own life right now and then commit to pray as Jehoshaphat did: "Lord, I don't know what to do but my eyes are on you."

DANIEL

An Ambassador for God

*I*n the years after the Northern Kingdom of Israel was conquered by the Assyrians, God continued to send His prophets to the Southern Kingdom of Judah, warning that they, too, would be carried away into bondage if they didn't repent and return to Him.

Prophets like Jeremiah, among others, faithfully delivered God's message while false prophets constantly reassured the people that God would never allow His city or His Temple to be destroyed as Jeremiah was predicting.

Many desperately wanted to believe that Judah would be spared.

After all, Judah was still standing 100 years after the Northern Kingdom had fallen.

But in 605 BC, Nebuchadnezzar's armies appeared at the gates of Jerusalem just as Jeremiah had predicted; and the world, as Judah had known it, was completely turned upside down.

The book of Daniel chapter 1 records what happened when the Lord delivered Jehoiakim, king of Judah into the hand of his enemy Nebuchadnezzar. The king of Babylon not only plundered the city, but in verse 3, Scripture says he…

> ³ … *ordered Ashpenaz, chief of his court officials, to bring into the king's service some of the Israelites from the royal family and the nobility—* ⁴ *young men without any physical defect, handsome, showing aptitude for every kind of learning, well informed, quick to understand, and qualified to serve in the king's palace. He was to teach them the language and literature of the Babylonians.* ⁵ *The king assigned them a daily amount of food and wine from the king's table. They were to be trained for three years, and after that they were to enter the king's service.*
>
> ⁶ *Among those who were chosen were some from Judah: Daniel, Hananiah, Mishael and Azariah.* ⁷ *The chief official gave them new names: to Daniel, the name Belteshazzar; to Hananiah, Shadrach; to Mishael, Meshach; and to Azariah, Abednego.*

Can you imagine how disorienting this was for Daniel and his friends?

They went from being princes in Judah to being hostages of a pagan king and his wicked purposes.

They were completely cut off from their homeland. Every hope they'd had for their futures was totally dashed.

They must have wondered, 'What in the world is going on?'

Michele Telfer

Nebuchadnezzar had some very specific purposes for his new captives.

He began by assigning them food from his own table.

Not only would that soften their resolve to resist their captivity, but it would also serve to separate them from their religious roots that were anchored in the Jewish food laws.

He also commanded that they be reeducated in the ways of the Babylonians and be forced to speak their captors' language.

Even their very names were changed from names that had glorified the living God of Israel to those that glorified the gods of their abductors.

Daniel was now called Belteshazzar; Hananiah became known as Shadrach; Mishael, Meshach; and Azariah was given the name Abednego.

Every element of Nebuchadnezzar's training was designed to emphasize his power over these young men.

He aimed to separate them from all they'd known and to press them into the mold of the world in which they were now living — the godless, pagan world of Babylon.

He had no thought for their desires, their hopes, or their well-being except as it ensured their usefulness to him.

But God had His purposes, even in this!

Over the years the Babylonians would take three groups of captives from Judah; and shortly after Daniel's group had been taken, the prophet Jeremiah wrote a letter to those now living in Babylon to encourage them in their trials.

He reminded them of the message God had given them through his preaching: that their exile was going to last for 70 years before they would be allowed to return. And he told them to settle down in Babylon, build houses and vineyards, marry and have children.

He told them to pray for and seek peace for their new home until then.

And he reminded them of God's heart for them in Jeremiah 29:11-13: *11 For I know the plans I have for you," declares the Lord, "plans to prosper you and not to harm you, plans to give you hope and a future. 12 Then you will call on me and come and pray to me, and I will listen to you. 13 You will seek me and find me when you seek me with all your heart.*

Everything the Lord allows in our lives is for a good purpose — to bless us and not harm us, to bring us closer to Him and cause us to seek Him.

You see, these Jewish captives in Babylon would be the ones who would one day return to rebuild the Temple and re-establish the nation.

By sending them to Babylon, God was preserving them as a remnant for His purposes, in a sense He was protecting them from the harsh judgment that was falling on those left behind in Judah.

It may surprise you to know that many Bible scholars believe that Daniel was only around 15 years old when he was taken captive; and yet Daniel responded to his radically changed circumstances in a remarkable way.

Daniel 1:8 reveals...

8 But Daniel resolved not to defile himself with the royal food and wine, and he asked the chief official for permission not to defile himself this way.

There is no sign that Daniel gave in to either bitterness or despair.

He simply determined in his own heart how he was going to conduct himself in these new circumstances.

He purposed that he would not defile himself by partaking of the king's wine or meat ('delicacies' according to some versions).

Have you ever wondered why he chose to resist the food, given all the other pagan oppressions being forced upon him?

Daniel knew that the Jewish laws about food were meant to identify him as belonging to God.

He knew that much of what he would be served would be unclean according to those laws.

He also recognized that the food coming from the king's table would have been sacrificed to pagan gods before it reached their plates.

Eating the king's food was participating in and identifying with the culture in ways he simply could not do.

He would not compromise his identity as a child of God, no matter the consequences.

Can you imagine the courage it took to refuse the provision the king had personally selected for them?

"But Daniel resolved not to defile himself' … and to trust God despite what had happened to him and his friends.

And God was at work because verse 9 reveals that God...

> *⁹ ... caused the official to show favor and compassion to Daniel, ¹⁰ but the official told Daniel, "I am afraid of my lord the king, who has assigned your food and drink. Why should he see you looking worse than the other young men your age? The king would then have my head because of you."*

> *¹¹ Daniel then said to the guard whom the chief official had appointed over Daniel, Hananiah, Mishael and Azariah, ¹² "Please test your servants for ten days: Give us nothing but vegetables to eat and water to drink. ¹³ Then compare our appearance with that of the young men who eat the royal food, and treat your servants in accordance with what you see." ¹⁴ So he agreed to this and tested them for ten days.*

The following verses reveal that God honored Daniel and his friends for their faithfulness, for not only were they healthier than their fellow trainees at the end of the 10 days but God gave them even more skill and wisdom than the others.

And as they entered the king's service, verse 20 tells us: "In every matter of wisdom and understanding about which the king questioned them, he found them ten times better than all the magicians and enchanters in his whole kingdom."

What grace God shows us! for as we honor Him, He will honor us.

I love how this chapter ends. Daniel 1:21 says that *"And Daniel remained there (in the Kings service) until the first year of King Cyrus."*

That covers the entire span of the captivity — the rest of the 70 years Jeremiah had prophesied! (Cyrus was the ruler who released the people to return to Jerusalem and rebuild the Temple.)

Daniel began with a determination to be faithful in the midst of his trial — and he continued in that faithfulness for the rest of his life.

We would do well to learn from him.

Though our circumstances may be very different – I am sure that many of us know what it is to have our hopes for the future shattered in some way.

And many of us have experienced great hardship that has not been of our own making.

However, our choice is the same as that of Daniel and his three friends: will we choose to turn away from the Lord in bitter regret, or will we seek Him with all our hearts and serve Him wherever He has planted us?

As He did with Daniel, God will give the grace to sustain us and accomplish His purposes in and through us, even in the most trying circumstances we face.

Daniel 2 relates another instance of God's grace and faithfulness. One night, Nebuchadnezzar had a troubling dream; and anxious to know what it meant, he called together all of the wise men and sorcerers in his employ.

He suspected they might not tell him the truth of the dream out of fear for their lives; so he devised a test to reveal if they were really hearing from their gods.

He refused to tell any of them what the dream itself had been insisting that if they were truly wise they would not only be able to tell him what the dream had been, but also what it meant!

This was an impossible task; and when they had no answer for him, Nebuchadnezzar decided to put all of the wise men in his kingdom to death — and that included Daniel and his three friends.

Daniel urgently asked his friends to pray.

He knew that God was the only One who could give the king the answers he needed.

So they did. They prayed fervently, and God revealed to Daniel both the dream and its meaning.

When Daniel appeared before the King, he was careful to give all the glory to God. He told Nebuchadnezzar that: "No wise man, enchanter, magician or diviner can explain to the king the mystery he has asked about, [28] but there is a God in heaven who reveals mysteries."

Daniel also told him that God had revealed the mystery to him "not because (Daniel had) greater wisdom than anyone else alive", but because God wanted the king to know what his dream meant.

Our God is the God of Heaven who wants to reveal Himself to us! What grace!

He doesn't hide Himself away like the false gods of Nebuchadnezzar's magicians.

He doesn't remain silent — rather He makes Himself known to those who seek Him.

The book of Romans reminds us that He first revealed Himself in creation, in the things His hands made.

The book of Hebrews reminds us that in times past He spoke through His prophets, further revealing His nature and His purposes.

And then, in what Hebrews calls "these last days," He has finally and completely revealed Himself to us through His Son, the Lord Jesus Christ.

God has always reached out in love to make Himself known to all people everywhere.

We see that here. God revealed the dream to Daniel not only to save the lives of the four young men from Judah but also so that a proud, pagan king might be introduced to the Living God.

So…what did Nebuchadnezzar see in his dream?

He saw an enormous statue with a head of gold but with its torso, arms, legs and feet made of different materials.

Then the entire statue was destroyed by a huge stone from heaven that grew to cover the entire earth.

And what did it mean?

God was showing Nebuchadnezzar not just his own immediate future, but the future of the world to come.

Nebuchadnezzar's kingdom was the head of gold; but it would be replaced by others.

However, no kingdom of men would endure. All would eventually come to an end and only the kingdom that came from heaven would remain.

It was the ultimate "big-picture" vision for this proud man to grasp and at least momentarily, he recognized Daniel's God to be the Living God who rules and reigns among men.

And he humbly prostrated himself before the 17-year old captive he'd thought to use for his own purposes!

Though young, Daniel was already showing himself to be the servant of God, not just the servant of the king!

This was not the only encounter, though, in which a king glimpsed the power of the Almighty God through Daniel's life and testimony!

I would like us to look at one final glimpse of God's grace that came towards the end of Daniel's life, approximately 65 years after Daniel chapter 2.

Three generations of Babylonian rulers had come and gone.

And Daniel, now in his 80s, was still serving as one of the area governors.

But, as Nebuchadnezzar's dream had foretold, another empire had arisen; and Darius the Mede now ruled in Babylon.

When Darius set up his new administration, he placed Daniel in one of the three highest positions in the kingdom, putting him in charge of the other two governors and of the 120 local rulers (or satraps as they were known).

The king had so much confidence in Daniel's integrity that he was planning to promote him over the entire kingdom.

Of course, the other officials all quickly realized that with Daniel in charge there would be no opportunity to line their own pockets, or feather their own nests "because he was faithful" Beyond that, many of these men were likely Medes or Persians themselves who couldn't abide the prospect of being under an "outsider" from the previous government — especially one who came from a weak, defeated people group.

And so they decided to move against Daniel however, they could find nothing in his 65+ years of service to accuse him with.

Not one instance of dishonesty or unfairness or immorality. Nothing.

And what an indictment of the deviousness of the human heart because when Daniel's enemies could succeed in no other way, they manipulated the laws of the land and the thought processes of the king to work their purposes.

They went to the king behind Daniel's back and warned that he really needed to do something to unite his very large, diverse empire.

Their suggestion was that he issue a decree stipulating that no one could pray to any god but him for 30 days on penalty of death!

I understand that this may seem unusual to us, but it was not uncommon in those days for rulers to be considered as a god by those whom they ruled over and so the trap was set.

They even slyly suggested that Darius put the order in writing and sign it, because they knew only too well that once this was done "according to the law of the Medes and Persians" the decree could not be altered in any way, not even by the King himself!

Daniel responded just as the schemers had hoped. Daniel 6:10 explains…

> *¹⁰ Now when Daniel learned that the decree had been published, he went home to his upstairs room where the windows opened toward Jerusalem. Three times a day he got down on his knees and prayed, giving thanks to his God, just as he had done before.*

In full knowledge of the decree…

Daniel continued to pray openly to the Living God, just as he always had done since his youth.

Naturally, his adversaries were quick to report him to the King.

For his part, Daniel didn't protest their accusations nor did he fight against the edict.

The faithful, honest, innocent Daniel submitted to the sentence that had been pronounced — death in a den of lions.

And don't you know that even there in that pit amidst the ravenous lions, he continued praying, peacefully trusting God to either protect him or take him home.

However, inside the palace, it was a different story. Darius was beside himself.

He was horrified at what had been done to Daniel, but he was powerless to change the punishment and so the King spent a miserable night fasting and praying for this man he so admired.

Early the next morning, he ran to the pit and cried: "Daniel, servant of the living God, has your God, whom you serve continually, been able to deliver you from the lions?"

And he was astounded to hear Daniel's voice reply: "May the king live forever![22] My God sent his angel, and he shut the mouths of the lions. They have not hurt me, because I was found innocent in his sight. Nor have I ever done any wrong before you, Your Majesty."

Truly this is the grace of God: He is able to protect those whose hope is in Him, who serve Him from a pure and faithful heart!

Darius then issued a new proclamation — this one praising Daniel's God. In Daniel 6:26-27, Darius declared, "he is the living God and he endures forever; his kingdom will not be destroyed, his dominion will never end. [27] He rescues and he saves; he performs signs and wonders in the heavens and on the earth. He has rescued Daniel from the power of the lions."

How about you, my friend? Do you know this mighty, glorious God of grace who saves?

Please do not leave our study of His grace still unsure of your relationship with Him.

Daniel's experience in Chapter 6 foreshadows the death of the Messiah and it paints a picture of the Lord Jesus Christ.

Like Daniel, Jesus was falsely accused by men whose jealous, bitter hearts led them to twist the laws and manipulate the decision-makers to work their purposes.

Like Daniel, Christ made no protest or defense; He did not try to protect or deliver Himself as He was given over to death.

But unlike Daniel, Jesus wasn't rescued.

He was crucified, died and was buried. And during His three days in the tomb, He ravaged Hades, ending the power of death.

That is what Easter is all about! He destroyed death by His death!

And when His friends ran to His tomb early in the morning of the third day, they found He was alive!

Jesus Christ conquered death for us by dying on the cross for our sins and rising again so that we could have eternal life!

Glory to God for His grace! Glory to God for His salvation!

This section of the book of Daniel ends with Daniel continuing to serve and prosper in the reigns of both Darius and Cyrus, the king who allowed the people to return to Jerusalem. (Daniel 6:28).

He never did make it back to Judah.

Tradition says Daniel died in one of the palaces of the king, in the same land to which he had been taken captive as a 15-year old young man.

But there can be no doubt that Daniel fulfilled God's purposes for him...that God placed him in those very courts to be His ambassador.

Daniel's life of integrity, faithfulness and excellence brought the pagan kings he served face to face with the Living God and paved the way for the remnant to return to Jerusalem and reestablish their nation.

Above all, Daniel's life shows us that the grace of God is always present, even in the worst of circumstances, always working out His purposes for our good and His glory.

Over the past five chapters we have seen many glimpses of God's grace in these Old Testament figures, haven't we?

Through the life of Abraham we learned that God keeps His Word to us even when we stumble…that He blesses us when we choose Him over the world; and when we trust Him completely, He provides us with salvation.

Joshua revealed that God equips those He calls and gives us His promises to empower our obedience. He is with us even in the midst of the most difficult circumstances of life and brings a testimony out of the trial that He will use for good.

Rahab taught us that God prepares hearts to seek Him and includes in His family all those who put their trust in Him that He is far less concerned about our past than He is about our future; and that those who are marked by the blood of the Lamb of God are accepted as His.

Elijah proved that God speaks to His people through His Word and answers prayer in often miraculous ways.

But it's not all about our performance! He understands our frailty and He cares about us enough to work even in the silences of life!

In the life of Jehoshaphat God showed that He treats us as beloved sons. He allows us our choices and lovingly disciplines us to bring us back to His path.

He honors us when we honor His Word. And when we focus on Him and His glory, our battles will be His battles and He will fight for us.

And finally, this lesson from Daniel shows us that God is in control; and even when our world is turned upside down, He is always working to fulfill His purposes. Daniel also reminds us that God reveals Himself to those who seek Him. He gives wisdom to those who ask and is fully able to protect us as we serve Him.

I hope you will never again allow anyone to say that the God of the Old Testament is a mean, vindictive, uncaring God!

He is, always has been and always will be a loving, kind, generous and welcoming God who longs for us to be in relationship with Him.

Reflection and Discussion

God graciously chose Daniel to go to Babylon as part of His ongoing plan for His people. He answered Daniel's prayers for wisdom and protected him from the schemes of men as well as from the hungry lions.

Read over Daniel 1 & 2 and Daniel 6 asking God to speak to you.

- Think back through everything we learned about Daniel. What glimpses of God's grace did you see in his story?

- What spoke to you about the way Daniel chose to follow God even when his circumstances were so difficult to understand?

- If you were honest, how do you respond when a trial comes your way? Do you accept it as from God and ask His help with it, or do you get angry with Him for allowing it in the first place? How can you become quicker to respond in faith?

- What was the "big picture" perspective God gave Nebuchadnezzar through his dream? What did the king come to recognize about Daniel's God? How do you suppose your view of God affects your life? Your decisions? Your ability to handle disappointments and even opposition?

- We often turn to Jeremiah 29:11-13 as a promise of good things to come when it's really more a declaration of God's good character. He is telling us something about Himself in these verses…that His purposes for us are always good, always loving, and always lead to the accomplishment of His will. Unfortunately, "good things" don't always happen to us; but rather what does happen God will use for our good. As we seek Him in times of trial, He will draw near to us because He loves us. How could believing that help you right now in the circumstances you are facing?

- In what we studied of Daniel's life, we learned that prayer was his first priority and his settled practice. Can you say the same thing about your own life?

- Granted, tough situations often arise so quickly there isn't time to think, much less pray. How can you be prepared for those times? Is there something you can work into your life — some settled practice — that will enable you to meet those moments in faith and trust rather than fear?

- Daniel shows us two very important perspectives: the "big picture" of God's sovereignty and the "long view" in following Him. From his youth, Daniel consistently served God with great wisdom, courage and faithfulness. For over 60 years, he exercised his responsibilities to the king with an excellence and integrity that was obvious to everyone so that Daniel and Daniel's God were known and honored throughout the kingdom. Could the same be said about you? What do you hope people will remember about you and the God you love long after you've gone?

It might be a good thing to write down those things you want to be remembered for and then pray asking God's help in living them out.

Encounters with Grace
in the New Testament

NICODEMUS

We Can't Work Our Way to God

We previously studied the lives of six Old Testament people who faithfully followed God with the limited revelation they had, experiencing what we called "Glimpses of God's Grace" because the fullness of that grace in Jesus Christ was yet to come.

Their faith and obedience are all the more remarkable because of that!

They were, in effect, walking in the shadows, believing in what was to come though they didn't see or understand it completely.

And their stories dispel the idea that the God of the Old Testament is a God of wrath and condemnation for their lives showed us that God has always been a gracious God who reveals Himself and longs for us to know Him.

And then, when the time was just right, Christ came into the world, God in the flesh, full of grace and truth. So now we're going to look at the lives of six people in the New

Testament who actually met the Lord face to face; and I believe that what we learn from their encounters with Christ will teach us even more about His grace for us.

We're going to begin today with Nicodemus, a man who had a very challenging conversation with Christ. The account is in chapter 3 of John's Gospel. We get to know Nicodemus in the first verse:

> *¹ Now there was a Pharisee, a man named Nicodemus who was a member of the Jewish ruling council.*

The first thing we learn about him is that he was a Pharisee, which quite literally means "a separated one".

We also learn that he was a member of the ruling council, so he was a figure of some reputation and authority among the Jews in Jerusalem.

The Pharisees were known for their devotion to the Scriptures. They were recognized as the greatest teachers in Israel.

And in their fervor to "get things right" they had added many teachings to the Mosaic Law.

In fact, when Nicodemus became a Pharisee, he would have had to swear an oath before witnesses that he would keep every part of the law of Moses as well as the 600 or so other rules the Pharisees had added to God's Word.

Unfortunately, focusing on their own efforts to please God, filled many of them with a sense of pride and self-importance and they were known for deliberately separating themselves from anyone who did not abide by their rules.

You might remember that Jesus strongly condemned their inevitable hypocrisy in His ministry.

That being said, it would be unfair to paint all Pharisees with the same brush – some of them were genuinely seeking God and it seems that Nicodemus was one of those, for when Jesus came to the Temple in Jerusalem Nicodemus asked to meet with Him privately.

Verse 2 tells us …

> [2] *He came to Jesus at night and said, "Rabbi, we know that you are a teacher who has come from God. For no one could perform the signs you are doing if God were not with him."*

The fact that Nicodemus came to Jesus at night may be surprising; but in those days, it was often the custom to seek out a teacher at night, so as to have an extended time of discussion without the fear of being interrupted.

However, from what Nicodemus says, it does seem that he was coming to Jesus in secret. And note that he says "Rabbi, we know…."

I think that Nicodemus was there on behalf of others on the council to find out just who Jesus was – could He be the Messiah they had been waiting for?

This was early in Christ's ministry, but it had already become very plain to the religious leaders that there was something extraordinary about Jesus.

Nicodemus calls Him "Rabbi", complimenting Him in a way, acknowledging that He was a recognized teacher with His own followers.

Nicodemus also acknowledged that Jesus was able to perform miracles, confirming that no one could do so "if God were not with Him."

But Jesus' reply in verse 3 turned everything upside down for Nicodemus.

> ³ *Jesus replied, "Very truly I tell you, no one can see the kingdom of God unless they are born again."*
>
> ⁴ *"How can someone be born when they are old?" Nicodemus asked. "Surely they cannot enter a second time into their mother's womb to be born!"*

Jesus went right to the heart. He knew that if Nicodemus really wanted to understand who the Messiah was, he first needed to understand what Jesus had come to do ...

This proud, educated, Scripture-saturated Pharisee first needed to understand that he needed a savior and that it was impossible for him to make himself right with God by his own self-effort.

Faultless obedience to the law was an impossible burden to carry, but that was the only way to God Nicodemus knew.

No wonder he was confused when Jesus began to talk about being born again!

Nicodemus knew there was nothing a person could do to enter into their mother's womb a second time.

And that really was the point!

Nicodemus was so sure that he was responsible for his own salvation…and Jesus said, no…you can't make it happen. It has to happen to you.

You have to be born from above, by the Holy Spirit of God.

Jesus wanted Nicodemus to realize that there is no way a person can affect the type of change in their heart that God requires.

The kind of radical transformation needed for a person to be reconciled to God, was something only God Himself could accomplish!

Sensing Nicodemus' confusion, Jesus went on to explain...

> [5] ... *"Very truly I tell you, no one can enter the kingdom of God unless they are born of water and the Spirit. [6] Flesh gives birth to flesh, but the Spirit gives birth to spirit. [7] You should not be surprised at my saying, 'You must be born again.'*

There are different ways of looking at what Jesus said here.

In saying that we need to be "born of water and the Spirit" some scholars say Jesus is encouraging Nicodemus to see beyond physical birth to the spiritual birth we need to experience to truly understand God's Kingdom.

In that case, being "born of water" would refer to a woman's water breaking as she is about to give birth.

But I also want you to consider something else.

Being a Pharisee, Nicodemus was well acquainted with the whole idea of ritual baths. In fact, there was row upon row of them outside of the Temple for people to use before entering.

When a Gentile converted to Judaism, they would undergo this ritual cleansing in order to be "born again", if you will, as a Jew.

But even Jews frequently used these ritual baths to symbolically purify themselves from all unrighteousness.

Nicodemus would have been very familiar with this practice, which was meant to give someone a fresh start with God.

But in saying what He did, Jesus revealed that mere water wasn't sufficient to cleanse the soul.

The externals of religion could not resolve the real problem — the problem of sin.

For a person to have a fresh start with God, they need to be born again by the work of the Holy Spirit.

Jesus knew that many of the religious leaders were struggling to come to terms with what God was doing through Him.

He knew how threatened they felt and that they worried about how His ministry might affect their own standing in the community.

What they perhaps did not realize was that what God was about to do could not be stopped; and so Jesus used the wind as an example, gently saying to Nicodemus ...

> *8 The wind blows wherever it pleases. You hear its sound, but you cannot tell where it comes from or where it is going. So it is with everyone born of the Spirit."*
>
> *9 "How can this be?" Nicodemus asked.*
>
> *10 "You are Israel's teacher," said Jesus, "and do you not understand these things?*

Michele Telfer

In effect, Jesus wanted Nicodemus to understand that only the Holy Spirit could bring men into the kingdom and that His work could not be managed or defeated by men.

Think about the wind for a moment. We cannot see it, but we can feel its effects.

We can shut ourselves off from the wind by sheltering from it, or by closing the window, but we can't stop it from blowing.

And the religious leaders could no more stop what God was doing through Jesus, than they could stop the wind.

As a teacher, Nicodemus was highly esteemed in the eyes of men but he didn't know everything!

I can't help but imagine the wonder on Nicodemus' face as he struggled to make sense of all that Jesus was saying, but I think in this we learn something remarkable about God in that grace receives us as we are.

Jesus is not put off by our inability to understand…

He isn't put off by our tentative questioning in the middle of the night … He will receive us just as we are!

And if we seek Him, He will never turn us away. But He will also always lead us to the real issues we need to face.

Like Nicodemus, there are times we struggle to accept His Word, but Jesus wants us to understand that we do need to accept His authority. He continued:

> [11] *Very truly I tell you, we speak of what we know, and we testify to what we have seen, but still you people do not accept our testimony.* [12] *I have spoken to you of earthly things and you do not believe; how then will*

you believe if I speak of heavenly things? ¹³ No one has *ever gone into heaven except the one who came from* *heaven—the Son of Man.*

In the Old Testament, God had promised to send a deliverer known as the Messiah.

The Prophet Daniel revealed him by the title "the Son of Man".

He would be the anointed leader of God's people and in fact, the name Messiah means Anointed One in Hebrew. It becomes Christos when translated into Greek and Christ in English.

Many Jews mistakenly imagined that this promised one of God would be a political leader who would free them from Roman oppression, but God's plan was slightly different than man's!

The Messiah would set people free, but from the power of sin and He would rule over a heavenly kingdom.

As Jesus began to reveal both Himself and His mission as the long-awaited Messiah to Nicodemus, He began to speak to the dumbfounded teacher in a way that he would most certainly be able to understand, declaring in verse 14 …

> *¹⁴ Just as Moses lifted up the snake in the wilderness, so* *the Son of Man must be lifted up, ¹⁵ that everyone who* *believes may have eternal life in him."*
>
> *¹⁶ For God so loved the world that he gave his one and* *only Son, that whoever believes in him shall not perish* *but have eternal life. ¹⁷ For God did not send his Son*

into the world to condemn the world, but to save the world through him.

Though we might wonder what Jesus meant when he referred to the serpent in the wilderness, we shall soon see that by GRACE Christ spoke to Nicodemus in a way that he could truly understand.

As an avid student of the writings of Moses, Nicodemus would have been very familiar with this particular story from Scripture.

We need to look at Numbers 21:4-9 in the Old Testament for Jesus' words here to make sense. For this particular event in Israel's history is rich with spiritual symbolism relating directly to what Jesus wanted Nicodemus to understand.

Numbers 21:4 picks up the story when the people of Israel, recently delivered from Egypt, were still wandering in the wilderness...

> *⁴ They traveled from Mount Hor along the route to the Red Sea,⁽ᵂ⁾ to go around Edom. But the people grew impatient on the way; ⁵ they spoke against God and against Moses, and said, "Why have you brought us up out of Egypt to die in the wilderness? There is no bread! There is no water! And we detest this miserable food!"*
>
> *⁶ Then the Lord sent venomous snakes among them; they bit the people and many Israelites died.*

Israel grew impatient as they followed God, imagining that somehow a life of slavery had been preferable to a life of freedom.

God had provided all the food they could eat with manna raining down from the sky and quail that flew into the camp each night.

He had also miraculously given them water to drink, and yet they despised His provision.

They longed to go back to the slavery that He had delivered them from.

Interestingly, the symbol of the Egyptian Pharaohs' was a snake and so it was no coincidence that God sent snakes among them to remind them of how painful their life in servitude had been.

The bite of these serpents was deadly. Just like sin, its wages were death.

More than that, no remedy for the serpents' bite could be found within the realm of men.

The people were powerless to counteract its deadly effects and so, confessing their sin, the people went to Moses asking him to pray for them so that the Lord would "take the snakes away."

Aren't we so often like that, desperate for the intercession of others so that we can get out of a difficult spot?

God didn't take the serpents away – but He did provide the Israelites a remedy!

> [8] *The Lord said to Moses, "Make a snake and put it up on a pole; anyone who is bitten can look at it and live." [9] So Moses made a bronze snake and put it up on a pole. Then when anyone was bitten by a snake and looked at the bronze snake, they lived.*

There are several things we need to emphasize before we get to the meaning:

The remedy for the serpent's poison was given by God. It was not devised by man.

The serpent was made of bronze, a metal that was associated with God's judgment in Scripture.

This was a one-time symbol of judgment — no other version of this snake was ever made ... there was one, and only one!

To be healed was simple enough, but it was personal.

No one else could look at the bronze serpent for you ... this was something each individual had to do for themselves.

It was the only remedy. There was no "self-help" available that would cure the disease life would be given by an act of faith alone!

So, what was the picture God was painting then, that remains to this day?

What was the message Jesus wanted Nicodemus to understand from this illustration in Israel's history? Let's go back to John 3, verse 4:

> *4 Just as Moses lifted up the snake in the wilderness, so the Son of Man must be lifted up,[f] 15 that everyone who believes may have eternal life in him."[g]*
>
> *16 For God so loved the world that he gave his one and only Son, that whoever believes in him shall not perish but have eternal life. 17 For God did not send his Son into the world to condemn the world, but to save the*

world through him. [18] Whoever believes in him is not condemned, but whoever does not believe stands condemned already because they have not believed in the name of God's one and only Son.

Jesus wanted Nicodemus to understand that the story of the serpent in the wilderness foreshadowed Christ and His death on the cross as payment for our sin.

Jesus was going to be lifted high on the Cross so that those who were dying might look to Him and live.

He would always and forever be the only way of salvation.

But each person must respond for themselves in a personal act of faith.

Nicodemus may have secretly come to Christ under the cover of darkness seeking what he thought he needed to know about the Messiah but his true need was far greater than he imagined.

He needed new life. He needed to be born again, to start over, and he would have to look to Jesus as his Savior for that to happen.

The Messiah Nicodemus looked for was far more than a political ruler!

He had come to be a sinless substitute for mankind's sin!

The religious law that Nicodemus loved and so earnestly followed could never bring a person into the new life that God desired.

As Paul later would say in Galatians 3:24 "… the law was (merely) our tutor to bring us to Christ, … we (are) justified by faith."

Jesus is able to do what the Law could never do … by His sacrifice we can be born again spiritually and whoever believes in Him shall not perish but have eternal life!

Have you personally looked in faith to Christ's death on the cross as the only way that you can survive the deadly poison of sin?

For all of us who have looked … it has the power to transform us and give us new life!

The conversation between Jesus and Nicodemus that night seemed to end without any conclusion. But I want us to look at the transformation we see in Nicodemus' life after that night …

We next see him in John 7.

Jesus had returned to Jerusalem for another of the special religious holidays and by this time His popularity was growing.

He continued to make claims about Himself and God, that no one else would ever dare to do.

And what was even more troubling to the religious leaders, Jesus was able to back up what He said with miraculous works!

More and more people were talking about Him and so the Sanhedrin eventually sent out members of the Temple guard to arrest Jesus and bring Him before them.

In John 7:45 onwards we learn that these officers returned to the Sanhedrin empty-handed, confessing that they had not arrested Jesus because [46] *"No one ever spoke the way this man does…"*

This infuriated the Pharisees …

> [47] *"You mean he has deceived you also?" the Pharisees retorted.* [48] *"Have any of the rulers or of the Pharisees believed in him?* [49] *No! But this mob that knows nothing of the law—there is a curse on them."*

These officers knew that Jesus was like no other!

And though the ordinary people had begun to see Christ for who He was – the religious leaders had not!

In verse 48 they ask the rhetorical question: "Have any of the rulers or the Pharisees believed in Him?"

They were certain that no educated person had believed in Christ, but they were evidently wrong for by this time there were several members of the ruling council who had begun to change their minds in Christ's favor.

Among them was Nicodemus who urged the other members of the ruling council to listen to Christ for themselves …

> [50] *Nicodemus, who had gone to Jesus earlier and who was one of their own number, asked,* [51] *"Does our law condemn a man without first hearing him to find out what he has been doing?"*

Of course, they were not willing to do that – their minds were made up; and they even turned on Nicodemus at that point arrogantly implying that he was a fool who didn't know what he was talking about.

Many think this indicates a change in Nicodemus – that he had begun to understand what Christ had said to him and he was willing to publicly ally himself in some degree with

Christ, even though that might have dire consequences for his own future in society.

Finally, at Christ's crucifixion in John 19, we realize that Nicodemus and his friend Joseph of Arimathea had in fact become followers of Jesus.

Verse 38 reveals that …

> *[38] … Joseph of Arimathea asked Pilate for the body of Jesus. Now Joseph was a disciple of Jesus, but secretly because he feared the Jewish leaders. With Pilate's permission, he came and took the body away. [39] He was accompanied by Nicodemus, the man who earlier had visited Jesus at night. Nicodemus brought a mixture of myrrh and aloes, about seventy-five pounds. [40] Taking Jesus' body, the two of them wrapped it, with the spices, in strips of linen. This was in accordance with Jewish burial customs. [41] At the place where Jesus was crucified, there was a garden, and in the garden a new tomb, in which no one had ever been laid. [42] Because it was the Jewish day of Preparation and since the tomb was nearby, they laid Jesus there.*

Mark 15:43 confirms that: "Joseph of Arimathea, a prominent council member, who was himself waiting for the kingdom of God, coming and taking courage, went into Pilate and asked for the body of Jesus."

I think it's easy for us to miss just what an incredible act of bravery this was!

With no thought for themselves or what it would mean for their positions in society and on the ruling council, these two men publicly identified themselves with Christ at His death.

Though part of the Sanhedrin, they had not agreed to send Jesus to His death...And it seems that Nicodemus and Joseph of Arimathea had not only finally understood the words Jesus had spoken to Nicodemus on that rooftop — that the Son of Man must be lifted up like the bronze serpent in the wilderness so that men might be saved — they had come to believe it for themselves.

How do we know they understood?

Well, Matthew 27:60 tells us that the tomb in which they laid Jesus was actually Joseph of Arimathea's own tomb.

Yet it would have been very unusual for a wealthy person to purchase a tomb for themselves outside of Jerusalem's walls and so close to a major execution site.

I believe that tells us that these two men may have prepared ahead for what they knew was sure to happen.

There's another reason I say this.

Do you see there in verse 39 that "Nicodemus brought a mixture of myrrh and aloes, about seventy-five pounds"?

Such a large amount of embalming spices would have been impossible to organize quickly, which also seems to indicate that they had made special preparation ahead of time.

What these two men did fulfilled the promise of God in Isaiah 53:9, that His suffering servant (Jesus) would be assigned a grave with the wicked but with the rich at His death.

Jesus died between two thieves (with the wicked) and yet at His death He was buried in the unused tomb of a rich man.

The selfless dedication of Nicodemus and Joseph of Arimathea touches my heart. It all took place right in the midst of the Passover celebrations.

In fact, part of the urgency surrounding their request was because the Sabbath would begin at sunset and so Jesus' body had to be prepared for burial quickly.

However, touching the dead made a person unclean and barred them from participation in religious rituals.

These two men were trained Pharisees and this act would have gone against every fiber of their training yet we see them willingly put aside all of the strict legalism of their past, to openly follow Christ even if it made them unclean according to the law of Moses.

They chose to hold nothing back in their service of the Lord, fully aware of what that meant for their status within the community they'd been a part of for so long.

Nicodemus' encounter with Christ and the words Jesus said to him that night changed both him and his friend Joseph forever.

The same truth they experienced can change us too as we realize that:

God's grace receives us just as we are …

It speaks truth to us in ways that we can understand.

But grace is personal – it requires our response, our personal faith in Christ's sacrifice.

The transformation grace brings will draw us to worship and serve God with no thought for ourselves, just as it did Nicodemus.

May you encounter the God of all grace today, know Him as your personal Savior and lovingly follow Him, no matter the cost.

Reflection and Discussion

Nicodemus' encounter with Christ teaches us that God isn't put off by our tentative questioning in the middle of the night. If we seek Him, He will never turn us away but will receive us just as we are. He will speak to us in ways that we can understand, but He will also lead us to the real issues we need to face. In the case of Nicodemus we learn that we can't work our way to God - we all need a Savior!

The words Jesus spoke to Nicodemus that night changed both him and his friend Joseph forever, drawing both of them into a worship and service of God they had never known before even as strict Pharisees. Grace is personal – it requires our response; and as we also put our faith in Christ's sacrifice as the only way to be saved, our lives will be transformed too!

Read John 3:1-18; Numbers 21:4-9; John 7:45-52 and John 19:38-42 taking time to listen for God's voice.

- Why do you think it would have been difficult for Nicodemus to openly follow Christ the night he met Him on the rooftop?

- Has following Christ "cost" you anything? Have you lost relationships or standing in the community over

Him? Was that difficult for you? If so, why?

- What do you think made it so difficult for Nicodemus to understand what Jesus was saying to him?

- What was the real need Jesus wanted Nicodemus to understand he had? How hard do we struggle with acknowledging that same need?

- How has Jesus spoken to you in ways that you can understand? Has it always been through words, or has it also been through what He has done?

- How do you react to the term "born again"? Do you find it helpful to think about the transformation that happens when we believe in Christ?

- With regard to the passage in Numbers 21, we mentioned that there was no "self-help" remedy for the bite of the serpent in the wilderness. What kinds of "remedies" do you see people trying to apply today to the problem of sin and death?

- What stands out to you about the actions of Joseph and Nicodemus at the death of Christ? What do you suppose they were feeling at that point before Christ's resurrection?

- What was the most meaningful thing you learned about grace as a result of Nicodemus' encounter with Jesus?

Spend some time in prayer and ask God to speak to you this week in a way you will understand.

THE WOMAN AT THE WELL

God's Unlikely Choice

We are exploring six different people in the New Testament whose lives were radically altered when they encountered the fullness of the grace of God in the person of Jesus Christ. And they have so much to tell us.

In our last chapter we looked at Nicodemus, the religious teacher who learned that all his efforts to remain free of sin would never gain him the relationship with God he hoped for.

He learned that forgiveness could only come from being born again by the Spirit of God — a work only God could do.

Now we're looking at the transformation of a woman whose story is very familiar to most of us... the Samaritan woman who met Jesus at the well just outside the village of Sychar.

I love to teach about her because she reminds me in so many ways of my own story, for she also had wasted many years of her life looking for love and acceptance in all the wrong places!

To fully grasp how remarkable this encounter was, we first need to understand a little about the people group to which she belonged, the Samaritans.

The Samaritans came into being 100s of years before, when the 12 tribes of Israel were divided into two different kingdoms after the death of King Solomon.

Ten tribes formed the Northern kingdom called Israel with their capital city of Samaria and the remaining two tribes formed the Southern kingdom called Judah, whose capital was Jerusalem.

Both of these kingdoms would eventually fall to different foreign invaders, but at different times.

The Northern kingdom of Israel fell first, conquered by the Assyrians who brought in their own people to colonize their new territory.

It was a common practice, mostly done to weaken the conquered people. And that is exactly what happened.

Many of the northern Jews ended up intermarrying with the Assyrians and that intermarriage gave rise to the Samaritan people — who were racially part Assyrian, part Jewish.

To the southern Jews, this was a blatant act of political treachery and disobedience to God, whose law expressly forbade intermarriage with foreigners.

Because they were a people of "mixed blood" the Samaritans were despised by the pureblooded Jews.

They were openly cursed in the synagogues. In fact, the word "Samaritan" was one of the most hateful swear words a person could use.

Samaritan testimony was never accepted in a Jewish court of law and in the unlikely event a Samaritan sought to convert to Judaism, the request was refused, because the Jewish Rabbis believed that there was no way for these heretics to be saved!

In all fairness though, these feelings of hatred were mutual.

There were many other tensions between these two neighbors. Some were longstanding.

For example, they strongly disagreed as to where God should be worshipped.

The Jews maintained that true worship was only possible at the Temple in Jerusalem, where it had been offered for centuries.

Conversely, the Samaritans held that God should be worshipped on Mount Gerizim in their own territory, because that was the place that God had first laid out all the blessings of obedience that His people would enjoy in the Promised Land many years before. (You can read about that in Deuteronomy 11:26-29 and the following chapters)

Some tensions were more recent. Josephus, a Jewish historian of the first century, tells us of an incident that took place sometime between AD6 – AD9 when a group of Samaritans somehow gained access to the Temple in Jerusalem one night.

Knowing that priests would become ritually unclean if they came into contact with a dead body which would prevent them from leading worship in the Temple the Samaritans scattered human bones across the Temple porches and all through the sanctuary!

Josephus says that this desecration actually interrupted Passover that year and considerably raised the level of the enmity between the two groups.

By the time of Christ, the Romans ruled all of Judea; and the Jews lived in the area around Jerusalem and also in the far north of the country around the Sea of Galilee.

The Samaritans continued to live in the area just north of Jerusalem and immediately to the west of the River Jordan …

Consequently, their territory formed a kind of barrier for any Jew travelling from Jerusalem in the south to Galilee in the north of the country.

To travel through Samaria took about three days, but should a Jew be foolish enough to go that way, they could not count on receiving any help along the way from the local inhabitants.

In fact, the Samaritans would often go out of their way to make the journey as difficult for them as possible.

So understandably, the Jews avoided going through that region altogether by crossing to the eastern side of the Jordan River whenever they had to travel northwards!

John begins the account in John 4:1 …

> [1] *Now Jesus learned that the Pharisees had heard that he was gaining and baptizing more disciples than John—* [2] *although in fact it was not Jesus who baptized, but his disciples.* [3] *So he left Judea and went back once more to Galilee.*
>
> [4] *Now he had to go through Samaria.*

As Jesus' popularity grew, He chose to withdraw to the region of Galilee in the north.

Why do you suppose John would say that Jesus "had to" go through Samaria, if Jews usually went to great lengths to avoid it?

He had to go … because there was someone He had to meet and not only was that person a Samaritan, as if that were not bad enough – it was a woman!

> [5] *So he came to a town in Samaria called Sychar, near the plot of ground Jacob had given to his son Joseph.* [6] *Jacob's well was there, and Jesus, tired as he was from the journey, sat down by the well. It was about noon.*
>
> [7] *When a Samaritan woman came to draw water, Jesus said to her, "Will you give me a drink?"* [8] *(His disciples had gone into the town to buy food.)*
>
> [9] *The Samaritan woman said to him, "You are a Jew and I am a Samaritan woman. How can you ask me for a drink?" (For Jews do not associate with Samaritans.)*

Jesus sat down at the well in the unrelenting midday heat as the disciples went into town to look for food.

And though it was customary for women to draw water in the cool of the evening this woman came to the well in the fierce midday heat, while all others were sheltering from it.

Why do you suppose she did that?

I think the answer is obvious...she wanted to avoid the other women and chose to go when no one else would be there

She probably never expected to see anyone there…much less a man…and a Jew at that!

Little did she know He had gone out of His way to meet with her!

It may seem unimportant to us that He asked her for a drink, but it was rare for a Jewish Rabbi to speak to any woman publicly, much less a Samaritan woman!

In fact, according to Jewish custom, He would have become ceremonially unclean if He so much as touched the water pot that she had touched.

From what John tells us, it is plain the woman understood that, for she even asked Jesus: "You are a Jew and I am a Samaritan woman. How can you ask me for a drink?'"

And in an almost amusing instance of understatement, John explains for the sake of his Gentile readers that "Jews have no dealings with Samaritans."

But Jesus was no ordinary Jew!

I think there is more going on here than meets the eye as Jesus begins to engage in conversation with the woman.

She was so sure that He wanted nothing to do with her because of who she was, and yet He did!

She thought that any contact with her would defile Him somehow – and I wonder if we are any different?

Have you ever felt that Jesus is somehow too holy for you to approach?

Do you carry a burden with you that you feel certain Jesus would never want to touch?

Let me tell you, Jesus not only wanted to lift this woman's burden, He wanted to touch her heart also — and just as He did not reject her, He will not reject you!

Very gently, Jesus continued. He …

> [10] … answered her, "If you knew the gift of God and who it is that asks you for a drink, you would have asked him and he would have given you living water."

As we saw in our last lesson, God often speaks to people in ways that they can understand and He will use well-known or even everyday things to communicate deep spiritual truths to people.

In that dry and dusty land, not surprisingly He used water to convey a spiritual truth.

Most of the year the people of that region would draw water from cisterns that had been filled with rain water which then stood stagnant in the tank.

So, a very high priority was placed on what they called "living water" running water that welled up from a spring.

As the name "living water" suggests, they believed that it brought a life all of its own and it was highly sought after, especially as the kind of water they would use in their purification rituals.

This was not the first use of "living water" to indicate something supernatural.

In Jeremiah 2:13, God likened Himself to living waters when He warned His people about turning away from Him. There God revealed:

"My people have committed two sins: They have forsaken me, the spring of living water, and have dug their own cisterns, broken cisterns that cannot hold water."

In calling Himself the spring of living water, God is proclaiming Himself to be the source of life.

Only He can truly quench our thirst for love, acceptance and significance.

So when Jesus said He was able to give her "living water," He was in fact revealing Himself to be God.

But the woman didn't understand yet – she was thinking in earthly, not spiritual terms ...

> 11 "Sir," the woman said, "you have nothing to draw with and the well is deep. Where can you get this living water? 12 Are you greater than our father Jacob, who gave us the well and drank from it himself, as did also his sons and his livestock?"

I think she rather impertinently tries to shut down the conversation by asking if He thinks he's greater than Jacob who had given them the well in the first place.

The somewhat humorous answer to her question would have been, "Well, yes" — because Jesus is far greater than both Jacob and his well!

He is "The Well" that will never run dry the sustainer of life and the only one who can quench the deep thirst of her soul.

But Jesus very lovingly did not allow her to change the conversation.

Verse 13...

> *13 Jesus answered, "Everyone who drinks this water will be thirsty again, 14 but whoever drinks the water I give them will never thirst. Indeed, the water I give them will become in them a spring of water welling up to eternal life."*

> *15 The woman said to him, "Sir, give me this water so that I won't get thirsty and have to keep coming here to draw water."*

His offer is amazing. He promises to quench her thirst forever, no matter how deep it may be!

And He reveals that those who come to Him will be filled with the life that comes from Him — eternal life.

She may have been intrigued by what Jesus said, but her response was still focused on her immediate, physical needs.

She was so tired of trudging to the well in the heat each day to avoid the judgmental looks of the other women that she longingly asks for the water he offers so that she won't have to keep making the trip!

Jesus knew what was in her mind. But He also understood the real reason for her pain and He wanted to deal with that. And so, in verse 16...

^{16} He told her, "Go, call your husband and come back."

^{17} "I have no husband," she replied.

Jesus said to her, "You are right when you say you have no husband. *^{18} The fact is, you have had five husbands, and the man you now have is not your husband. What you have just said is quite true."*

And there was the heart of the problem.

This woman had been married to five different men and she was not even married to this sixth man she was with!

What could have happened?

Why so many broken relationships?

Had she just "been looking for love in all the wrong places"?

Or did she just have "bad luck" finding the right person?

Or could it have been because she was barren?

Could that have been the reason she felt such shame and was driven from relationship to relationship?

We don't know ... but we can certainly understand why she avoided the other women.

It's easy to judge other people when we don't know what's gone on in their lives, when we haven't had to walk in their shoes.

Just like the rest of us, I'm sure this woman was thirsting for love and acceptance with a desperate need to fill the emptiness inside and to belong.

But she had only met with failure!

The truth about grace is that it helps us to see ourselves as we really are; and if we will humbly agree with what God shows us, we will find that we can be forgiven and made whole again!

But this woman wasn't quite ready to do that. Look at the way she tried to redirect the conversation away from her sin and her need by focusing on the contentious issues of the day.

> *19 "Sir," the woman said, "I can see that you are a prophet. 20 Our ancestors worshiped on this mountain, but you Jews claim that the place where we must worship is in Jerusalem."*

Remember, the Jews and Samaritans disagreed as to where God should be worshipped.

Personally, I don't think she cared about who was right and who was wrong about that!

She knew that Jesus obviously had some insight into her life and her struggle (perhaps she wondered if someone else had told Him about her) …

Whatever the case, she quickly used a contentious topic to try to change the subject!

Jesus replied using the respectful form of address in those days, saying …

> *21 "Woman," … "believe me, a time is coming when you will worship the Father neither on this mountain nor in Jerusalem. 22 You Samaritans worship what you do not know; we worship what we do know, for salvation is from the Jews. 23 Yet a time is coming and has*

now come when the true worshipers will worship the Father in the Spirit and in truth, for they are the kind of worshipers the Father seeks. 24 God is spirit, and his worshipers must worship in the Spirit and in truth."

He addressed her politely, which is quite remarkable when you consider how others might have addressed her!

Jesus revealed to her that worshipping God is far more than a matter of where religious duties should be performed.

With His coming, the old things were taking on a new depth, a new meaning.

In verse 23 He revealed that the hour had arrived for people to worship God in the Spirit and truth that God the Father was seeking people who wanted a real relationship with Him.

Why does the need to worship in the Spirit and truth make so many uncomfortable?

I can almost feel how cornered she felt when, in one final attempt to evade Him:

25 The woman said, "I know that Messiah" (called Christ) "is coming. When he comes, he will explain everything to us."

The Samaritans used only the first five books of the Old Testament; and yet they too were expecting the promised Messiah – the Anointed One God had promised to send.

But whereas the Jews expected the Messiah to be a political deliverer the Samaritans expected Him to be a great teacher ... And so, she tries to end the conversation by saying, in effect:

"I do not understand all of this, but I do know that there is one coming who will help it all make sense. For the Messiah will explain everything …."

Then [26] *"Jesus said to her, "I who speak to you am He.""*

This is astounding!

It is the first time in His ministry that Jesus has been this explicit about Who He is.

And He chose to reveal that truth about Himself to a despised Samaritan woman.

You can almost sense the silence that fell on the conversation at that moment.

If this were a film, there would be closeups of the woman's incredulous face and Jesus looking intently at her.

And into that intense silence…burst the disciples with their lunch in verse 27.

Now I frequently sense in the gospels that the disciples' timing was a bit "off", and this certainly illustrates the point!

You can imagine them suddenly, and loudly, bursting in on this scene and startled by what they see, their voices suddenly die down.

They look at each other, wondering what's going on, but no one has the courage to say anything …

The tension was broken. And what did the woman do?

[28] *Then, leaving her water jar, the woman went back to the town and said to the people,* [29] *"Come, see a man who told me everything I ever did. Could this be the*

Messiah?" [30] *They came out of the town and made their way toward him.*

When she saw Christ for Who He Is, everything changed for her. John tells us that she even left her water jar at the well as she ran back to town.

Now, it may seem like such a small thing, yet think about it this water jar had controlled her life only moments before and yet, she leaves it behind, forgotten at the well, it is not that important after all!

Not only that, but she goes back to the people in the town — the very ones she had been so anxious to avoid before — to tell them all that has happened!

And that is the amazing thing about encountering the fullness of God's grace in Jesus Christ.

He alone has the power to free us from shame and from what has controlled us and the freedom His grace gives us is a testimony to share with others!

Her message is as simple as it is powerful: "Come, see a Man who told me all things that I ever did. Could this be the Christ?"

Do you notice she's not ashamed anymore?

In fact, she's willing to use her past life as the basis for her testimony!

And though the question she asks is a very simple one: "Could this be the Christ?" it is one that invites investigation and draws people to go in search of Christ for themselves.

There is so much that we can learn from her about how to share what Christ has done for us!

I marvel at Christ's kindness to this woman, for in doing what He did, Jesus entrusted the Gospel message to someone that no one else would have even spoken to!

The good news for you and for me is that God's choice of unlikely messengers hasn't changed, so there's room for us!

> *31 Meanwhile his disciples urged him, "Rabbi, eat something."*
>
> *32 But he said to them, "I have food to eat that you know nothing about."*
>
> *33 Then his disciples said to each other, "Could someone have brought him food?"*
>
> *34 "My food," said Jesus, "is to do the will of him who sent me and to finish his work. 35 Don't you have a saying, 'It's still four months until harvest'? I tell you, open your eyes and look at the fields! They are ripe for harvest. 36 Even now the one who reaps draws a wage and harvests a crop for eternal life, so that the sower and the reaper may be glad together.*
>
> *37 Thus the saying 'One sows and another reaps' is true. 38 I sent you to reap what you have not worked for. Others have done the hard work, and you have reaped the benefits of their labor."*

Are you as encouraged as I am that the disciples were still missing the point of what was going on?

They are so focused on the physical food they'd just bought, that they completely misunderstand what Jesus is saying.

Jesus is speaking about spiritual food, a spiritual sustenance that comes from doing the Father's will — sower and reaper working together to bring in a harvest of souls.

It is very likely that as He tells them to look at the fields that are ripe for harvest, He is pointing to the people of the town who are rushing towards them, wanting to see for themselves the truth of the Samaritan woman's witness.

Dressed in their light brown clothing, they may indeed have looked like ripened grain bobbing in the wind.

And this was just the beginning of that harvest.

Verse 39 …

> *39 Many of the Samaritans from that town believed in him because of the woman's testimony, "He told me everything I ever did." 40 So when the Samaritans came to him, they urged him to stay with them, and he stayed two days. 41 And because of his words many more became believers.*
>
> *42 They said to the woman, "We no longer believe just because of what you said; now we have heard for ourselves, and we know that this man really is the Savior of the world."*

Notice how this had become personal for them.

They had now heard His message for themselves and they recognized that Jesus is not only the Messiah, He is "the Savior of the world."

Not just of the Jews, or even half-Jews, but of the Gentiles also!

We learn so much about the grace of God in Christ from the Samaritan Woman. We learn that…

He sees every soul as valuable …He is seeking out every one of us, no matter who we are or what we've been.

He helps us to see ourselves as we really are, and it is there that we are made whole because once things are exposed, things can be healed.

And finally, the grace of God in Christ sets us free to share with others! We too, can work in His fields and bring in the harvest He so desires.

May it be so for all of us!

Reflection and Discussion

I marvel at Christ's kindness to the Samaritan woman at the well outside of Sychar. For the first time in His ministry, Jesus directly claimed to be the Messiah and in doing so He entrusted the Gospel message to a woman that no one else would have even spoken to!

The good news for you and for me is that God's choice of unlikely messengers hasn't changed, so there's room for us to be used in His Kingdom even today!

Read John 4:1-42 this weekend. Ask God to speak to your heart.

- The woman was so sure that Jesus wouldn't want to touch her water jar. Do you think that there are certain things in your life that Jesus would not want to touch – that if you brought them to Him he would be so shocked He would turn away? Do you really think you could defile Him in some way?

- What has this story of the Samaritan woman taught you about that? What struck you the most about the way Jesus dealt with her?

Michele Telfer

- The Samaritan woman had to acknowledge some truths about her own life in order to receive what Christ was offering her. For most of us, that can be pretty painful. Why do you think that kind of self-knowledge is a prerequisite to faith?

- How does it help you to know that Christ is truly "living water"? How does that image speak to you?

- Can you think of any "broken cisterns" you or those you love might have been drinking from?

- Do you think that you are often too practical for your own good? That you miss what the Lord is trying to say sometimes because you struggle to see things from a spiritual perspective"?

- In your experience, do people often hone in on contentious issues to try to avoid answering the uncomfortable questions God is asking them? How have you handled such "conversational maneuvers"?

- Why does the need to worship in the Spirit and truth make so many uncomfortable?

- Jesus entrusted the Gospel message to someone that no one else would have even spoken to! How does this encourage you?

- Many people feel intimidated when it comes to speaking to others about Christ. How would you describe the Samaritan woman's "evangelistic efforts"? What words come to mind? Did anything in particular stand out to you about her witness?

- Last week, we saw a somewhat gradual change in Nicodemus after he met Christ. The Samaritan woman showed a more immediate transformation. How would you describe the change in your life after coming to faith?

- Have you ever used your own testimony of God's grace to share the Good News with others? Why or why not? How did others respond?

Spend some time in prayer about your testimony and what God would have you share with others. It might help to write it down. Conclude by asking God to give you the opportunity to share it with someone.

JOHN THE BAPTIST

Faithful Until the End

*A*s we continue our series about people who had life-changing encounters with Christ in the New Testament, I want us to look at a relative of Jesus who had a very important part to play as God's plan for salvation unfolded.

Because he was a part of Christ's extended family, his encounter with Christ differed from that of Nicodemus or the Samaritan woman we have already studied. But we can learn much from how he experienced God's grace in his own life.

We don't often think about it, but the New Testament opens at a dark time in Israel's history.

God's people had been dominated by the Roman Empire for many years and yet they had not lost hope in God's promise in the Old Testament to send the Messiah, the one who would deliver them and usher in the kingdom of God.

However, they mistakenly believed that the promised Messiah would set them free from Roman oppression; but God had a far greater freedom in mind for His people — He was going to set them free from their bondage to sin!

God had also promised that the Messiah would be preceded by a prophet who would announce His arrival.

By this time, there had been 400 long years of silence since any of God's prophets had spoken and weariness was beginning to set in.

Then one day it happened!

The voice of a prophet began to be heard in the Judean wilderness, calling people everywhere to repent and prepare for the coming of the Lord.

That voice belonged to John the Baptist, a cousin of Jesus.

John's parents were Zecharias and Elizabeth. They were both from the tribe of Levi, the tribe responsible for conducting Israel's worship.

Elizabeth was a relative of Mary, the mother of Jesus.

You might remember from the story of Christ's birth that Mary visited her cousin Elizabeth after the angel Gabriel's announcement to her.

Zecharias, or Zechariah as he is sometimes called, was a priest who served from time-to-time at the Temple in Jerusalem Luke 1:6 tells us that both Zecharias and his wife "were righteous in the sight of God, observing all the Lord's commands and decrees blamelessly" but verse 7 then says [7] ... they were childless because Elizabeth was not able to conceive, and they were both very old."

In those days, most people associated barrenness with a lack of God's favor; but Luke makes their devotion to God plain.

One day, as Zecharias was serving in the Temple in Jerusalem, an angel of the Lord appeared to him, announcing that his prayer for a child had been heard and that his wife Elizabeth would bear him a son despite their advanced age.

The angel declared that the child was to be called John and that "many (would) rejoice because of his birth, [15] for he (would) be great in the sight of the Lord.

The angel also said that John was to be specially devoted to the Lord in that he was "never to take wine or other fermented drink" and promised that John would "be filled with the Holy Spirit even before he (was) born."

This was a truly remarkable statement, for up until this time only kings and prophets were anointed with God's Spirit … and none of them had ever had the Holy Spirit come upon them in the womb.

John would be an extraordinary son, born under extraordinary circumstances; and the angel declared that he would " … turn many of the children of Israel to the Lord their God" for he was to "make ready a people prepared for the Lord."

Can you imagine how startling this announcement would have been to the elderly Zecharias? But it is such an example of how God's grace works, ordering things in every detail even before the event itself!

You see, John's birth was no accident — and neither was yours, no matter how it came to pass.

Now I appreciate that some might have difficulty relating to this but Psalm 139:13-16 says that each individual one of us is known intimately by God and has been precious in His sight before we ever drew a single breath.

> *13 For (it was He who) ... knit (you) together in (your) mother's womb...*
>
> *15 (your) frame was not hidden from (Him) when (you were) made in the secret place,...*
>
> *16 (His) eyes saw (your) unformed body; (and all the days ordained for (you) were written in (His) book before one of them came to be.*

You and I are not here by accident! We are here because God wanted us and brought us into life.

He loves us and He has a purpose for our lives. We are not now, nor have we ever been, outside His grace.

Luke then tells us that his parents named him John as the angel had commanded and "the child grew and became strong in spirit; and he lived in the wilderness until he appeared publicly to Israel."

The Gospel of Mark picks up his story; and chapter 1:4-8 reveals how John's ministry began:

> *4 And so John the Baptist appeared in the wilderness, preaching a baptism of repentance for the forgiveness of sins. 5 The whole Judean countryside and all the people of Jerusalem went out to him. Confessing their sins, they were baptized by him in the Jordan River. 6 John wore clothing made of camel's hair, with a leather belt*

around his waist, and he ate locusts and wild hon-ey. ⁷ And this was his message: "After me comes the one more powerful than I, the straps of whose sandals I am not worthy to stoop down and untie. ⁸ I baptize you with[ᵃ] water, but he will baptize you with[ᵇ] the Holy Spirit."

As far as preachers go, John was rather unusual! And actually, so was his message!

And yet do you see how effective his ministry was: "all the land of Judea, and those from Jerusalem" went out to hear him speak and more than that, they responded to his message!

He preached in one of the harshest environments on earth — the desert wilderness of Judea!

It was an uncomfortable place of scorching heat —and yet still people flocked to hear him speak.

He didn't look successful; he didn't "look the part" really.

Truth be told, he seemed rather strange with his "clothing made of camel's hair" and his odd diet.

And if you read further, you'll see he never tried to cleverly "sell" his message or cater to what his listeners wanted to hear either.

In fact, he called his listeners a "Brood of vipers" in Luke 3:7 — and yet people still responded to his message!

John was not a people-pleaser; and yet his ministry bore such great fruit… why?

Because he was faithfully delivering the message God had given him by the power of the Holy Spirit, that there was One coming who was much more powerful than he — the Messiah, who would baptize people not with water but with the Holy Spirit.

But it seems he didn't know all the details.

We read his testimony in John 1:29-37 …

29 The next day John saw Jesus coming toward him and said, "Look, the Lamb of God, who takes away the sin of the world! 30 This is the one I meant when I said, 'A man who comes after me has surpassed me because he was before me.' 31 I myself did not know him, but the reason I came baptizing with water was that he might be revealed to Israel."

32 Then John gave this testimony: "I saw the Spirit come down from heaven as a dove and remain on him. 33 And I myself did not know him, but the one who sent me to baptize with water told me, 'The man on whom you see the Spirit come down and remain is the one who will baptize with the Holy Spirit.' 34 I have seen and I testify that this is God's Chosen One."[a]

35 The next day John was there again with two of his disciples. 36 When he saw Jesus passing by, he said, "Look, the Lamb of God!"

37 When the two disciples heard him say this, they followed Jesus.

It amazes me that though John would have known Jesus as his cousin, he did not know that Jesus was the Messiah he was actually proclaiming, even when Jesus was beginning His ministry!

But when John saw the Spirit of God resting on Jesus in the form of a dove, he knew exactly what that meant.

His cousin Jesus was God in the flesh, the promised Messiah; and from that moment on, he boldly declared Him to be the "Lamb of God" who had come into the world to be our great sacrifice for sin the One who had "surpassed" him "because he was before him."

I think the main take away is this: John didn't know the full story when he began to proclaim the Messiah's coming.

John knew He was coming — but he didn't know exactly who He was going to be.

However, God's plan was unfolded to John as he walked in obedience to God's call. That obedience enabled John to fulfill his part in God's plan.

Notice, too, that John's mission was about connecting people to Jesus, not to himself.

When people asked him if he was the Christ, John would clearly tell them "No"!

In fact, he maintained that he was not even worthy to untie Christ's sandal — the task of the lowliest household servant.

And when Jesus came to him to be baptized in Matthew 3 "John tried to prevent Him" saying that if anything Christ should be the one to baptize him!

He repeatedly revealed Jesus to be the One people should follow and even happily allowed his own disciples to become Christ's disciples instead.

In fact, John 3:27-30 relates that when some of his own disciples were worried that Christ was gaining in popularity over him, John

> "... replied, "A person can receive only what is given them from heaven. [28] You yourselves can testify that I said, 'I am not the Messiah but am sent ahead of him.' [29] The bride belongs to the bridegroom. The friend who attends the bridegroom waits and listens for him, and is full of joy when he hears the bridegroom's voice. That joy is mine, and it is now complete. [30] He must become greater; I must become less."

John always pointed people to Christ and away from himself.

That is something we all have to do ...

Make no mistake — it's a blessing to be used by God in someone else's life but we must remember that He must increase and we must decrease for He alone is able to save.

He alone is the giver of life.

And there is something else we can learn from this great servant of God.

He didn't compromise the truth of God's message even when he knew it would likely lead to the end of his ministry.

John knew the deep need for mankind to repent or turn from their old lives of sin to Christ as their Savior and he was willing to bring that message to even the most powerful politicians of that day.

Remember, at this time Herod the Great ruled Judea as Rome's puppet king.

Herod was a terrible man who killed anyone who threatened his authority, even his own family members!

When he died, shortly after the birth of Christ, he split the kingdom among his sons so that none of them would ever be as great as he was.

They may not have been as great, but they were as horribly immoral as their father had been.

One of those sons named Herod Antipas divorced his wife in order to marry his niece Herodias.

There was just one small problem however: Herodias was still married to his brother, Phillip!

Rather than ignore what was going on, we are told in Luke 3 that John rebuked Herod Antipas for the evil things he was doing, but especially for what he was doing with his brother's wife…

John faithfully declared the message that God had given him, no matter who was in the audience.

Calling them to repentance, he urged both Herod and Herodias to make their hearts right with God.

As could be expected, the outcome of that confrontation was not good for John. Matthew 14:3-4 simply states that …

> [3] … Herod had arrested John and bound him and put him in prison because of Herodias, his brother Philip's wife, [4] for John had been saying to him: "It is not lawful for you to have her." [5] Herod wanted to kill John,

but he was afraid of the people, because they considered John a prophet.

I want us to stop here for a moment. While John was languishing in prison, he apparently began to struggle.

Matthew 11 describes John's conflict. Verse 2...

> *² When John, who was in prison, heard about the deeds of the Messiah, he sent his disciples ³ to ask him, "Are you the one who is to come, or should we expect someone else?"*

> *⁴ Jesus replied, "Go back and report to John what you hear and see: ⁵ The blind receive sight, the lame walk, those who have leprosy[b] are cleansed, the deaf hear, the dead are raised, and the good news is proclaimed to the poor. ⁶ Blessed is anyone who does not stumble on account of me."*

For John to struggle with doubt is remarkable to me!

Remember, he'd had a special conception and birth.

He had been filled with the Holy Spirit from before he was born.

John certainly heard from God throughout his life!

He'd seen Jesus and recognized Him as the Messiah.

He had humbly and faithfully preached the message God had given him, whether it was popular or not and he'd seen people turn from their sin to follow the Lord.

Yet in the darkness of his prison cell, John's heart began to question whether or not Jesus really was the Messiah!

Why would he do that?

Well, remember people had been expecting a political deliverer … one who would come to set them free from the Romans (and from the wicked rule of the various Herods).

We don't know for sure, but perhaps John had also been hoping that Christ would have started a revolution by now and that surely once Jesus was on His ancestor David's throne in Jerusalem, all would be well.

But nothing like that was happening; and so John began to doubt.

This seems hard for us to believe that such a man of God would do this, until we look at our own lives!

For when the Lord doesn't do things in the way we expected him to, or in perhaps the way we'd hoped, it is sometimes hard not to question Him.

But even in that dark moment, Jesus had no rebuke for John …

Rather he sent John's disciples back to him with a reassurance reminding John that He was doing the very miracles that Scripture had said the Messiah would do…the very signs that proved the kingdom of God had indeed come among men.

And then he encouraged John to stand fast and not stumble in his faith simply because his expectations were not being fulfilled.

What I love about the gracious way Jesus deals with this situation is that He then turns to the crowd to commend John to them, despite his questioning, despite his doubts.

7 As John's disciples were leaving, Jesus began to speak to the crowd about John: "What did you go out into the wilderness to see? A reed swayed by the wind? 8 If not, what did you go out to see? A man dressed in fine clothes? No, those who wear fine clothes are in kings' palaces. 9 Then what did you go out to see? A prophet? Yes, I tell you, and more than a prophet. 10 This is the one about whom it is written:

"'I will send my messenger ahead of you, who will prepare your way before you.'[c]

11 Truly I tell you, among those born of women there has not risen anyone greater than John the Baptist; yet whoever is least in the kingdom of heaven is greater than he.

Jesus reminds the people of just who John the Baptist was — a prophet sent by God.

But he wasn't just any prophet as they'd known in the past. He was the prophet whom God had said would prepare the way for the Messiah. And Christ used the words of Malachi 3:1 in which God tells the Messiah that He would send a messenger before Him to prepare the way for His coming.

In saying this Jesus is not only commending John as the forerunner …

He is also proclaiming Himself to be the Messiah — the ruler of God's Kingdom everyone had been waiting so long for.

I hope John's disciples carried those words back to him as well. What reassurance this would have given him, hearing those very words from the lips of Christ Himself.

God's grace reached out to John in the midst of his darkness, and that encourages me greatly

because it helps me to realize that God's love for us is not diminished when we struggle with our circumstances or with doubt.

He understands and meets us where we are…if we seek Him with our whole hearts.

So how did John the Baptist complete his ministry for the Lord?

We saw earlier that Herod wanted to kill John, but wouldn't do it because he feared the people who believed John was a prophet.

That wasn't good enough for Herodias though. She began to nurse a grudge against John for what he had said about her and wanted him dead.

However, Mark 6:20 and onwards reveals that she wasn't able to get to him…

> 20 *because Herod feared John and protected him, knowing him to be a righteous and holy man. When Herod heard John, he was greatly puzzled; yet he liked to listen to him.*

Herod wouldn't give in to her demands for vengeance. In fact, he often brought John out of his cell and conversed with him.

It may sound strange but it was not unusual in those days for a ruler to bring a captive in to talk to them but one can only imagine Herodias' growing anger as she realized that the king liked to listen to the preacher she despised!

When given an opportunity, she was quick to act!

> [21] *Finally the opportune time came. On his birthday Herod gave a banquet for his high officials and military commanders and the leading men of Galilee.* [22] *When the daughter of[b] Herodias came in and danced, she pleased Herod and his dinner guests.*
>
> *The king said to the girl, "Ask me for anything you want, and I'll give it to you."* [23] *And he promised her with an oath, "Whatever you ask I will give you, up to half my kingdom."*

This girl's name was Salome and as soon as she heard Herod's drunken offer she knew she needed to speak to her mother …

> [24] *She went out and said to her mother, "What shall I ask for?"*
>
> *"The head of John the Baptist," she answered.*
>
> [25] *At once the girl hurried in to the king with the request: "I want you to give me right now the head of John the Baptist on a platter."*
>
> [26] *The king was greatly distressed, but because of his oaths and his dinner guests, he did not want to refuse her.* [27] *So he immediately sent an executioner with orders to bring John's head. The man went, beheaded John in the prison,* [28] *and brought back his head on a platter. He presented it to the girl, and she gave it to*

her mother. ²⁹ On hearing of this, John's disciples came and took his body and laid it in a tomb.

John the Baptist and King Herod couldn't have been more different.

The prophet of God didn't care what people thought of him, it only mattered what God thought of him …

By contrast, Herod — who cared nothing for God —was only concerned about saving face in front of his friends!

And so, against his better judgment, he allowed the prophet of God John to be executed!

Matthew tells us that when Jesus heard of His cousin's death, He withdrew to a solitary place.

I think it's obvious that Jesus loved John and his death mattered a great deal to Him.

It reminds me of what we are told in Psalm 116:15: "Precious in the sight of the Lord is the death of his faithful servants."

John the Baptist was faithful to the very end of his life. He fearlessly preached the message God had entrusted to him.

How did he find the strength to do that? He found it in the grace of God.

GRACE enabled John to finish his course and complete the work he had been called to do – even though in the world's eyes, it seemed that his life ended in failure and death.

We need to experience this grace in our own lives. When things come to an end that we may not have anticipated or desired.

God's grace can help us shift our perspective.

Instead of feeling abandoned or deprived, we can trust that God's purposes for that season in our lives have been completed and He is leading us on to the next step.

So what can we learn from the life and death of John the Baptist?

First of all, he was faithful to God's call he promoted Christ rather than himself and drew people to Jesus rather than his own ministry.

He was a man like us; and at his lowest point, he had his questions, his doubts. But he took them to the right place and found the answers his heart needed.

And when his ministry came to an end, it was not because he'd failed God or because he'd overstepped the mark in challenging the lifestyle of a politician…

No, it came to an end because God called His faithful servant home, his work complete. He finished well.

Oh, the grace of God that sets us apart even before we are born and unfolds God's plan to us as we walk in obedience to His call that encourages us and gives us the strength to hold on even when we doubt and yes, the grace of God that enables us to finish our race and to finally hear those words from our Lord: "Well done, good and faithful servant".

Reflection and Discussion

This week we studied the life of John the Baptist, who was a relative of Jesus. Though his encounters with Christ were different than those of Nicodemus and the Samaritan woman, there was much to learn from God's grace as evidenced in his life.

It was by grace that John was set apart even before he was born. Grace unfolded God's plan to him as he continued to walk in obedience to His call. It was grace that encouraged him in his dark night of doubt and uncertainty in prison and gave him the strength to hold on. Ultimately, God's grace enabled John to finish his race and finally hear those words we all long to hear from the Lord: *"Well done, good and faithful servant"*.

Begin by reading Luke 1:5-25 and Mark 1:4-8 this weekend. Ask God to speak to your heart.

- John the Baptist is one of the most unusual followers of Christ we meet in the New Testament. If someone asked you to describe him, what words or phrases would you use?

- What struck you the most about the circumstances of his birth as recounted in Luke 1:5-25?

- Scripture says that John was specially chosen by God before he was born, even to the point of being filled with the Spirit in Elizabeth's womb. What do you think that says about the sanctity of human life itself and the question of when life begins?

- Read Psalm 139:13-18 and share what stands out to you about who we are even before birth. What does it mean to you that you are not a random accident?

- Jesus said to His disciples in John 15:16: "You did not choose me, but I chose you and appointed you so that you might go and bear fruit — fruit that will last…." That statement applies to all of us who follow Him. How do Jesus's words comfort you? Challenge you?

- What did you learn from John's attitude about Christ's growing popularity in John 3:27-30? What did his response reveal about him? John was humble; and yet he was also confident that he was doing what God had told him to do and content to remain in that calling. How do those two things work together?

- My father maintained that he didn't want to follow God because there were some things about God he just didn't understand; but what did we learn from the way that John the Baptist followed God in John 1:29-37 without having all of his questions "nailed down"?

- Read Matthew 14:3-4 and Matthew 11:2-11. Like John in prison, we might find ourselves in a very difficult situation — one in which we don't fully understand what God is doing. What encouraged you in his sending questions to Jesus through his disciples?

What did you think of the way Jesus responded to him?

- What do you learn from John when it comes to handling those dark nights of the soul? Where do you go when your questions arise? Have you ever experienced receiving that kind of reassurance from the Lord?

- Read Mark 6:20-29. John was willing to speak the truth no matter the cost to him personally. To those on the periphery, his death may have seemed a waste, the result of an unwise confrontation with the king. Was it really a disastrous way for his ministry to end? How do you suppose God viewed it?

- What is the most meaningful thing you are taking away from this look at John the Baptist?

Spend some time in prayer asking God to give you the same boldness as John the Baptist.

MARY AND MARTHA

His Love for You is Never in Question!

As we continue in our New Testament study of people who encountered God's grace in the person of Jesus Christ, we will be looking at the amazing interactions between Jesus and a certain family who had befriended Him.

Today's lesson includes one of my favorite sections of Scripture where the revelation of God's grace is so powerful that I know it will affect us deeply.

Lazarus and his sisters Martha and Mary lived in Bethany just two miles from Jerusalem.

They were close friends of Jesus, and He frequently stayed with them when visiting the Temple.

The first time we meet Martha and Mary is in Luke 10:38-42, where Luke describes some initial tension between the two sisters ....

> *38 As Jesus and his disciples were on their way, he came to a village where a woman named Martha opened her home to him. 39 She had a sister called Mary, who*

sat at the Lord's feet listening to what he said. [40] But Martha was distracted by all the preparations that had to be made. She came to him and asked, "Lord, don't you care that my sister has left me to do the work by myself? Tell her to help me!"

[41] "Martha, Martha," the Lord answered, "you are worried and upset about many things, [42] but few things are needed—or indeed only one. Mary has chosen what is better, and it will not be taken away from her."

Martha's name meant "lady of the house" or "mistress" and she certainly seemed to be in charge as she is the one to open their home to Christ.

Martha often gets criticized for her busyness but I think that many of us can identify with her because if Jesus came to our house we, too, would want everything to be in order for Him.

Martha was a hard worker and while there's nothing wrong with that we are told she resented her sister for listening to Christ's teaching rather than helping her in the kitchen

In those days, few rabbis would have allowed a woman to sit at their feet and learn from them.

And yet Jesus not only welcomed Mary's devotion, He was not willing to push her out to help with the cooking.

Instead, Jesus lovingly helped Martha to see that she was worried about things that in the end had no eternal value as His teaching had.

Michele Telfer

Martha often comes off poorly in comparison with her sister Mary; but God continued to work in her heart, as is evidenced in what happened in John 11 when Lazarus was deathly ill.

Verse 1 …

¹ Now a man named Lazarus was sick. He was from Bethany, the village of Mary and her sister Martha. ² (This Mary, whose brother Lazarus now lay sick, was the same one who poured perfume on the Lord and wiped his feet with her hair.) ³ So the sisters sent word to Jesus, "Lord, the one you love is sick."

These two women loved Jesus. They knew that God had anointed Him most powerfully and that He not only spoke with authority, but He was able to perform miracles as well!

So when their brother Lazarus fell terribly ill, their first thought was to immediately send for Christ to ask that He heal him.

As the story opens, Jesus was on the other side of the Jordan River, a full day's journey from Bethany.

We are told that upon receiving the sisters' message, Jesus told the messenger that …

⁴ … "This sickness will not end in death. No, it is for God's glory so that God's Son may be glorified through it."

And then He did a very unexpected thing. John tells us in verse 5 …

5 Now Jesus loved Martha and her sister and Lazarus.6 So when he heard that Lazarus was sick, he stayed where he was two more days, 7 and then he said to his disciples, "Let us go back to Judea."

It is worth noting that Jesus did not say that Lazarus would not die — He merely promised that this tragic situation would not end in death.

And whereas I am sure the messenger immediately returned to the sisters, eager to give them the good news, Jesus delayed two more days before going to their aid.

We will soon discover that by the time Jesus arrived in Bethany, Lazarus had been dead for four days.

If you work out the timing, that means that Lazarus must have died soon after the messenger had set out.

Think about it:

- Day one — the messenger travels to Jesus, and Lazarus dies soon after he left.

- Day two — the messenger returns to the sisters while Jesus stays where He was.

- Day three — Jesus waits yet another day before setting out.

- Day four — Christ arrives in Bethany and is told that Lazarus has been dead four days!

And that makes me wonder what the sisters thought of the messenger's report when he got back to Bethany on that second day?

Can you imagine the sadness they must've felt when the messenger rushed in with the news that "Jesus says: 'this sickness will not end in death!'" and their beloved brother was already gone?

I imagine the sisters and their friends had many questions about the message Christ had sent.

If He was the Messiah as they had hoped, how could He have been so wrong about things? How could He not have known?

They must also have wondered why Christ didn't immediately return with the messenger.

What did that indicate about His love for them?

For though John is careful to tell his readers that "Jesus loved Martha and her sister and Lazarus" they surely struggled to understand why He had not quickly intervened. Why had He delayed?

- Isn't that so like us, when God allows an unexplained circumstance to arise in our own lives and we also wonder why God has done nothing to intervene?

- At times like that I like to remind myself that His love for me is never in question!

- I have come to believe with all my heart that His grace is at work even when our world is shattered and it seems that He doesn't care.

When Jesus told the disciples that they were going to Bethany, they voiced their concerns. The Jewish leaders had recently tried to stone Christ, so Jerusalem and the surrounding area was extremely dangerous for Jesus.

Jesus reassured them and explained "Our friend Lazarus has fallen asleep; but I am going there to wake him up."

12 His disciples replied, "Lord, if he sleeps, he will get better." 13 Jesus had been speaking of his death, but his disciples thought he meant natural sleep.

Though His disciples knew only that Lazarus was ill, Jesus knew that Lazarus had died.

But He also knew that He was going to raise him from the dead. That's why He likened His friend's death to sleep – as something temporary.

I love how the disciples didn't understand at this point. Somehow it encourages me to see they struggled to realize Christ's power.

Jesus didn't leave them in their confusion. Verse 14...

14 So then he told them plainly, "Lazarus is dead,15 and for your sake I am glad I was not there, so that you may believe. But let us go to him."

16 Then Thomas (also known as Didymus[a]) said to the rest of the disciples, "Let us also go, that we may die with him."

Jesus knew that His disciples' faith would be strengthened by what they were about to witness.

And He admitted to being glad "for their sakes" that He had not been in Bethany so that they might see and believe that indeed nothing is impossible for Him!

And so they headed to Mary and Martha's house.

186 |

John picks up the story in verse 20...

> [20] *When Martha heard that Jesus was coming, she went out to meet him, but Mary stayed at home.*

> [21] *"Lord," Martha said to Jesus, "if you had been here, my brother would not have died.* [22] *But I know that even now God will give you whatever you ask."*

Martha's actions here show us just how much her priorities had changed.

There was a new urgency in her relationship with the Lord.

She had some deep questions that needed answering and she wasn't going to wait to bring them to Jesus.

She was the first one to go out to meet Christ. Her personality hadn't changed, just its focus.

We can almost hear her heartbreak and regret as she declares "if you had been here, my brother would not have died."

I don't think this is an accusation as much as it was one of those comforting statements those in grief repeat to each other over and over again as they struggle to deal with their loss.

I can imagine Mary and Martha consoling themselves with such an expression.

But even in the midst of her loss and confusion, Martha addresses Jesus as "Lord" using a term that essentially meant: "my owner", "my leader"

And by faith she insists: [22] *But I know that even now God will give you whatever you ask."*

It's perhaps true that Martha wasn't exactly sure what Jesus could do in the situation…but she was convinced that He could do whatever He willed!

He promised her in verse 23 ….

> 23 … *"Your brother will rise again."*
>
> 24 *Martha answered, "I know he will rise again in the resurrection at the last day."*
>
> 25 *Jesus said to her, "I am the resurrection and the life. The one who believes in me will live, even though they die;* 26 *and whoever lives by believing in me will never die. Do you believe this?"*

Martha knew they would see Lazarus in the final resurrection when the dead are raised on the Day of Judgement…but that was the only resurrection she knew about.

Then Jesus spoke an even greater hope into her hurting heart, promising eternal life for all those who believe in Him.

And that is the most important grace we encounter in the Person of Jesus Christ.

He is the life and the resurrection we all so desperately need.

This physical life we have is not the whole story because it is only temporary — God has provided eternal life to those who believe in Jesus.

That is the hope He gave Martha; and His words to her on that painful day have comforted millions of believers since.

And I love how she answers Him:

27 "Yes, Lord," … "I believe that you are the Messiah, the Son of God, who is to come into the world."

Martha declares with certainty that Christ is the promised Messiah! She understands!

She then immediately runs to find her sister Mary, telling her that Jesus is asking for her.

How that touches my heart — because we see that even in the midst of her own grief, Martha wanted others to know the hope that is in Christ.

Mary, followed by their visitors from Jerusalem, went out to Him and in her anguish, she reiterates what her sister had said only moments before: "Lord, IF You had been here, my brother would not have died."

There are no great words of faith from the woman who had sat at His feet — only tears of grief.

And filled with compassion...

33 When Jesus saw her weeping, and the Jews who had come along with her also weeping, he was deeply moved in spirit and troubled. 34 "Where have you laid him?" he asked.

"Come and see, Lord," they replied.

35 Jesus wept.

36 Then the Jews said, "See how he loved him!"

37 But some of them said, "Could not he who opened the eyes of the blind man have kept this man from dying?"

Do you know that verse 35 "Jesus wept" is the shortest verse in the Bible? And yet how powerful it is!

Jesus saw the heart-wrenching pain caused by death and even though there were some murmuring against Him in the crowd, He wept with compassion!

But, let me suggest that Jesus may also have been weeping for Lazarus because He knew that He was about to call him back from the place of blessing!

I think we often incorrectly focus on physical life being the most important blessing of all!

Several years ago, I became seriously ill and was taken to hospital by ambulance. When I was admitted, a doctor and two nurses acting as witnesses, asked for my end-of-life decisions, as they really did not expect me to live.

As they filled in the paperwork, I remember quietly whispering to God that I did not want to die. I had a husband I deeply loved and two children still in high school at the time.

The Lord suddenly and clearly spoke a thought into my mind: "All of your days were written in my book before one of them came to be. Just because you have heard the doctor's concern, it does not mean that you have one day less than you ever did".

I felt a calm come over my heart from that point on.

Obviously, I was restored to health, as I'm here to tell you the story today!

But I remember the first time I returned to church after being in hospital for so long.

During one of the worship songs I started to cry as I sensed the powerful presence of God.

But though I was so grateful to still be with my family, I am still not sure if I was crying out of gratitude to be alive, or if I was crying out of regret because I was not with the Lord in Heaven!

Because of that experience, I am not sure if Jesus was crying for the grieving sisters and their friends, or if He wept for Lazarus, whom He was about to call back from the place of blessing.

Regardless, His tears show us that grace feels our pain and that God is moved by our suffering!

No one could have imagined what Jesus was about to do! Verse 38 …

> *38 Jesus, once more deeply moved, came to the tomb. It was a cave with a stone laid across the entrance. 39 "Take away the stone," he said.*

"But, Lord," said Martha, the sister of the dead man, "by this time there is a bad odor, for he has been there four days."

At that time the Jews believed that the soul remained near the body for three days after death in the hope of returning to it and they even used to carve a small window into their tombs for the soul to depart through after that time had elapsed.

It has been mentioned several times in our text that this was now the fourth day Lazarus lay dead.

Everyone present knew that not only was Lazarus dead, any hope they had held on to of that ever changing was gone forever!

No wonder Martha was concerned by Christ's command to take away the stone.

> *40 Then Jesus (reminded her), "Did I not tell you that if you believe, you will see the glory of God?"*

As Jesus thanked God the Father in advance for answering His prayer, those present dutifully removed the stone.

Then in a loud voice, Jesus commanded:

> *43 ... "Lazarus, come out!" 44 The dead man came out, his hands and feet wrapped with strips of linen, and a cloth around his face.*

Jesus said to them, "Take off the grave clothes and let him go."

There is so much to take note of here!

Let me begin by asking, if Jesus was going to raise Lazarus with a command, why not command the stone to roll away too?

And why would Jesus ask those present to remove the graveclothes when He surely did not need their help?

I believe it is evidence of His love for us, how He invites us to be involved, to join Him in the work that really only He can do!

Though it is by God's grace that we are delivered from death He invites His followers to be stone-movers and grave-clothes un-wrappers!

He invites us to help remove whatever obstacles stand in the way of someone responding to His call and to assist one another to live free of all that once bound us!

If you're like me, you may well be wondering what that looks like in day-to-day life.

In my experience, the first step in doing any of this is to look at my own heart and life. Am I the example I should be?

Do my attitudes and actions express His love, His kindness, His grace? Can others look at me and see Him?

And then we must pray! Only the Holy Spirit can set someone free.

We are never to barge into someone's life with our words or actions, no matter how well intentioned.

Before we ever speak a word, we need to pray specifically that the Spirit would remove whatever might be holding someone back from responding to Christ.

And we do the same for our brothers and sisters who are in Christ.

We all need the loving assistance of other believers to step into the abundant life that God has planned for us. We cannot do it alone.

So, we remind each other of what the Scriptures say.

We forgive each other when we fail.

We strengthen each other when burdens become too heavy and when faith begins to weaken.

Gently, humbly and cheerfully, we follow Him together and watch those grave clothes slip away.

When I teach about Mary and Martha, people often ask me why I think Jesus delayed — why He allowed this hardship in the lives of three people He obviously loved when He could have prevented it.

Jesus allowed this to happen so that the disciples' faith could be strengthened. He knew they would need that because of what was soon to follow.

When we face something we would far rather not deal with, we would do well to remember that it's not always about us. Sometimes our pain is used as a catalyst for God's wider purposes as it was here.

Do you remember at the beginning of this passage Jesus had promised that Lazarus' "… sickness (would) not end in death. … (and that it was all) for God's glory (because) God's Son (would) be glorified through it."?

Many people think that Jesus was talking about the miracle He was about to do in raising Lazarus, but God's plan was far greater than even that!

This miracle of raising Lazarus from the dead was the event that finally led the religious leaders to send Jesus to the cross where our salvation was purchased and God was glorified in the face of His enemies.

John tells us that many who saw Lazarus' resurrection believed in Christ…

> [46] *But some of them went to the Pharisees and told them what Jesus had done.* [47] *Then the chief priests and the Pharisees called a meeting of the Sanhedrin.*

"What are we accomplishing?" they asked. "Here is this man performing many signs. [48] If we let him go on like this, everyone will believe in him, and then the Romans will come and take away both our temple and our nation."

Though they feigned concern at how the Roman's might respond to Christ's growing popularity, the religious leaders were more worried, I think, about losing their own authority.

And so when the High Priest Caiaphas pronounced that it was better that "… one man die for the people than … the whole nation perish" their plot to kill Jesus was set in motion.

Because of this, Jesus and His disciples withdrew from Bethany to a city called Ephraim on the edge of the wilderness, but because all Jewish males had to do be in Jerusalem for Passover

Jesus returned to His friends in Bethany once more and a celebration was given in His honor …

John reveals in John 12:2 that at that dinner Martha served, while Lazarus was among those reclining at the table with him. *3 Then Mary took about a pint[a] of pure nard, an expensive perfume; she poured it on Jesus' feet and wiped his feet with her hair. And the house was filled with the fragrance of the perfume.*

What a joyous occasion this must've been!

We haven't mentioned Lazarus much in the lesson, but wouldn't you like to know what he was thinking and feeling?

Both sisters sought to bless Christ for what He had done for their family in raising their brother from the dead.

Mary gave her most treasured possession, pouring a bottle of highly valuable perfume, worth over a year's wages, on His feet and the fragrance of her perfume filled the house with its loveliness.

Martha gave her gift of loving hospitality — and the delicious aroma of her cooking was no less precious or welcome!

Both of their offerings were "sweet smelling offerings to the Lord" — their gratitude was just expressed in different ways.

But it was also a sad occasion in many ways.

Within days Jesus would be arrested and crucified.

How precious it must have been for these three friends of Jesus to look back afterwards on this meal and reflect on the One who loved them and poured out His grace upon them so miraculously.

We have seen so much in the lives of Mary and Martha, the sisters of Lazarus of Bethany.

What have they shown us about God's amazing grace? They have shown us that...

Grace is at work even when our world is shattered and it seems as if God doesn't care. His love for us is never in question.

This physical life we so desperately cling to is not the whole story because it is only temporary — God by His grace has provided eternal life to those who believe in Jesus Christ for He is the life and the resurrection we all so desperately need.

Grace feels our pain and God is moved by our suffering. He weeps with us but more than that He invites us to join Him in the work that only He can do, removing obstacles that keep people from believing and helping each other lay aside the things that bind us and keep us from following Him.

Loved ones, I think many of you know that I have faced my fair share of grief in these last years with the sudden death of my beloved husband so what I share with you today I know to be true in a very personal way.

In any life there will be times of heartache. There will be times that we struggle with the unexplained, but know this: God's love for you is never in question.

True hope is found in the person of Jesus Christ and when we turn to Him He can use our pain for His purposes!

My prayer for us today is that we learn to trust Him and that we will grow in His grace as we face all that life brings.

Reflection and Discussion

Mary, Martha and Lazarus were close friends of Jesus; and I'm sure that when Lazarus fell sick and died, the two sisters were left with many questions about Christ's love for them. However, from their story in John 11 we learn that grace is at work even when our world is shattered and when it seems as if God doesn't care. His love for us is never in question. True hope is found in Jesus Christ, for He has provided eternal life to all who believe in Him. He is the life and the resurrection we so desperately need.

We also learn that God feels our pain and is moved by our suffering. But more than that, if we are willing to turn to Him in our struggles, He will use those very circumstances in ways that we could never have imagined.

Begin by reading Luke 10:38-42 and John 11:1—12:6. Ask God to speak to your heart.

- We aren't told much directly about Mary's personality in these Scriptures, but Martha's temperament is very much on display. How would you describe her? What particular strengths and weaknesses do you see in her?

- What did Jesus help Martha see about herself?

- Like Martha, do you sometimes feel that you're worried about too many things and not focused on what really is important? Do you sometimes find yourself resentful of those with different gifts or ways of serving? Who was Martha really criticizing in her complaint?

- What do you infer about Mary's personality from the things we've seen in the lesson? What do you imagine were her strengths and weaknesses?

- It's important to notice that Jesus wasn't criticizing Martha's personality or elevating Mary's. What do you think He was really speaking to?

- Mary and Martha were different, but neither was less valuable than the other in God's Kingdom. He uses all of us — indeed, He needs all of us with our amazing differences. How can we grow in our ability to work with each other?

- Did you identify with Mary and Martha's grief? How might you have struggled with delayed answers to prayer or the pain of the unexplained? (This does not have to be about the death of a loved one — there are many kinds of loss.)

- What did it mean to you that Jesus wept?

- How did Christ's words to Martha about eternal life speak to you? Have His words helped you in the face of loss or grief?

- In what ways does God keep our eyes on Him during trials?

- What are some "obstacles" that keep people from believing in Christ? How might we help remove them?

- How might we help each other gain freedom from the things that keep us bound — from habits or thoughts or sins we cannot seem to shake? What kind of attitudes do you think would be necessary to do that for each other?

- Was it helpful to see how the resurrection of Lazarus was a part of God's greater plan? How so?

- Do you have a story to share about how God has used a trial in your own life, or in someone else's, to minister to others and accomplish things for His Kingdom?

Spend some time in prayer asking God to help you to trust Him, even in unexplained circumstances. Ask Him to help you always remember that His love for you is never in question.

PETER

~~~

The God of Second Chances

*P*eter was one of the most important characters of the New Testament. He's also one of my favorites.

Because he lived and ministered alongside Christ, he would have encountered God's incredible grace on a daily basis. The Gospels and the book of Acts are full of his experiences.

And if there's one life in which we see the transformative power of God's grace at work, it is Peter's!

Peter originally went by the name Simon. He lived in Capernaum and was a fisherman along with his brother Andrew and his friends James and John.

In fact, he was doing just that when his life took a different direction.

Matthew 4:18 says that Jesus found Peter and his brother Andrew by the Sea of Galilee and called to them "Come, follow me … and I will send you out to fish for people."

Luke 5 adds that they were washing their nets on the shore after an unsuccessful night of fishing.

Jesus got into Simon's boat and asked him to put out from the land a little so that He could better speak to the large crowd that was following him.

After speaking to the crowd...

> *4... he said to Simon, "Put out into deep water, and let down the nets for a catch."*
>
> *5 Simon answered, "Master, we've worked hard all night and haven't caught anything. But because you say so, I will let down the nets."*
>
> *6 When they had done so, they caught such a large number of fish that their nets began to break. 7 So they signaled their partners in the other boat to come and help them, and they came and filled both boats so full that they began to sink.*

I love the fact that Simon Peter was willing to let down the nets again despite the fact that they were exhausted and had given up work for the day!

He was willing to obey Christ — even though "common sense" surely said it would be wasted effort!

And that one act of obedience changed everything!

Verse 8 tells us...

> *8 When Simon Peter saw this, he fell at Jesus' knees and said, "Go away from me, Lord; I am a sinful man!" 9 For he and all his companions were astonished at the catch of fish they had taken...*

In that moment, the proud, self-sufficient, skeptical Simon Peter saw in Christ, a goodness, a "rightness" far beyond his own.

And he was brought to his knees before Him.

Jesus said to Simon, "Don't be afraid; from now on you will fish for people." *11 So they pulled their boats up on shore, left everything and followed him.*

Consider the challenge Christ gave them here…

He would teach them to fish for people instead of fish!

I am touched by their immediate willingness to leave everything to follow Him.

If only we would be as quick to follow Him when He calls!

But their response was not without a certain element of risk! It required faith.

Simon not only walked away from the large catch that day. He walked away from the only life he'd ever known in order to become something he'd never been.

He'd been a successful fisherman — what kind of "fisher of men" would he turn out to be? And what did that even mean?

Throughout all the following gospel accounts, we see Peter on that journey.

He followed Jesus imperfectly, in fits and starts, sometimes getting the point, sometimes not — responding to Christ's gentle and not-so-gentle rebukes, receiving His forgiveness and redirection more times than we can count. And don't we see ourselves in his story!

We're going to briefly look at just three of his many experiences as he became who Christ had called him to be.

The first occurred during one of the high points of his spiritual journey when they were at a place known as Caesarea Philippi.

The location is significant because it was a place where false gods had long been worshipped.

There was a famous water-filled cave there where people worshipped the Greek god Pan — the god associated with wild nature, shepherds and flocks.

In fact, human sacrifices often were thrown into that cave from the top of the cliff leading many to believe that it was a gateway to hell itself!

But Pan was not the only false god worshipped there.

Herod the Great had constructed a marble temple dedicated to the worship of the Roman Emperor just outside the cave; and there were many other altars to false gods carved into the cliff face as well!

In truth, a person could not think of Caesarea Philippi without thinking of all the gods there were to choose from!

It was here that Jesus asked His disciples a critical question — a question that would mark the turning point of His whole ministry!

Everything prior to that day was in preparation for the question He asked them here and everything after that day was in preparation for the cross.

So, what was the question?

According to Matthew 16:13 Jesus began by asking His followers: "Who do people say the Son of Man is?"

As He did at other times, Jesus referred to Himself as the Son of Man, which was a title for the Messiah coming from the Old Testament writings of the Prophet Daniel.

Notice that Jesus first asks who other people say that He is.

And the disciples reveal some of the current theories people had about Him, answering: "Some say John the Baptist; others say Elijah; and still others, Jeremiah or one of the prophets."

Though everyone agreed there was something quite different about Jesus, there was much speculation among the people about who He might really be.

And then Jesus asked the twelve the critical question that would change things forever: [15] "But what about you?" … "Who do you say I am?"

Simon Peter was the only one to answer Him. In verse 16 he said, "You are the Messiah, the Son of the living God."

I love that Jesus made it such a personal question; for in the end, what really matters is not what others say about Jesus, but rather who we personally know Him to be.

It's a question each of us must answer for ourselves.

Peter's reply reveals that though he might not have fully understood everything about Christ, he knew that all the opinions people had of Him were inadequate and fell far short of the truth.

Peter knew that Jesus was more than any prophet and in declaring Him to be the Son of the Living God, Peter was, in fact, acknowledging that Jesus was equal to God Himself.

Can I just say that Jesus' response to this statement is critical? You see, if He was not divine, if he was merely a good teacher or a good person, as a faithful Jewish man, Jesus would have been obligated by the Law of Moses to correct Peter for speaking heresy.

But Jesus did not correct him! Instead …

> [17] *Jesus replied, "Blessed are you, Simon son of Jonah, for this was not revealed to you by flesh and blood, but by my Father in heaven.* [18] *And I tell you that you are Peter,[b] and on this rock I will build my church, and the gates of Hades[c] will not overcome it.*

We first need to note that according to Jesus own words in verse 17, it is God the Father Himself who has revealed this truth to Peter's heart.

This wasn't just Peter's normal impulsiveness. God had communicated Himself to Peter and made Himself known.

There is something else here though that we must be sure not to miss.

Do you see in verse 17 that Jesus first called him by his given name, Simon, son of Jonah? And then by the name Peter in verse 18?

Why did Jesus use both names?

Perhaps it was to remind Peter of their very first encounter years earlier.

John 1:42 tells us that when Andrew first brought his brother Simon to Jesus — before they left their nets to follow Him as we saw in Matthew 4 and Luke 5 — Jesus had looked at him and said, "So you are Simon, the son of John? You shall be called Cephas (which means Peter)."

As John explained there, Cephas and Peter mean the same thing — "rock" — one is the Aramaic word and the other the Greek.

Some scholars have pointed out that there wasn't any recorded use of the name Peter among Jewish families. So Jesus was giving him a "new" name, a name that indicated something very important about him.

And from that day on, he was known as Simon Peter. Simon the Rock.

It could be that Jesus is saying here in Matthew 16, "Do you remember what I called you? What I said you were to be?"

What did Jesus say to him as Peter in verse 18?

> *18 And I tell you that you are Peter,[b] and on this rock I will build my church, and the gates of Hades[c] will not overcome it.*

We know there are differences among Christians as to what exactly Christ meant here; but I think we can all acknowledge that at the very least, that Jesus was marking Peter out in a unique way in this text.

He was the first disciple to openly confess Christ as the Son of God.

And in the years to come he would be chief of the apostles, their acknowledged leader, the one who first preached at Pentecost, the one who opened the kingdom to the Gentiles and the one who led the early Church as it grew and expanded

And in the ages since, every individual who has personally declared Jesus as the Messiah, the very Son of the Living God, who has made the same discovery as Peter, is another stone added into that eternal building that is the Church.

Standing before the massive rock face and the water-filled cavern known as a gateway to Hell that was associated with so many false gods and religions, …

Jesus pointed out the true rock and declared that the Church He would build on it would be both indestructible and victorious.

The fact that there is still an historical body of Christ existing since the time He founded it, that there are believers in every nation in the world proclaiming the gospel and being salt and light is proof of Christ's words here.

Every barrier Satan has put in the way, every offensive he has mounted, every fortress he has built has not been able to withstand the presence and the preaching of the Church of Jesus Christ.

The enemy's efforts ultimately fail. The Church does not — and will not.

What grace! From the very beginning, Jesus not only saw Peter for who he was, but also for who he would become. And here in Matthew 16, He reminded His somewhat unstable disciple of the name he'd been given and He gave him a glimpse of the role he would play that would call those things out of him.

But the path of true discipleship and transformation has many bumps along the way; and Peter still had some to encounter.

In amongst his moments of great faith, he also had moments of great failure. Let's look at one of those.

In Luke 22 we are invited to look in on a very precious time of fellowship that Jesus had with His closest followers.

On the night before He was arrested, Jesus and His twelve disciples gathered for a dinner that has come to be known as the Last Supper.

When they arrived at the borrowed room, Jesus tenderly washed the feet of all 12 from the grime of their journey.

The King of King and Lord of Lords humbled Himself, taking on the role of the lowliest servant in the house, to do what no one else had been willing to do!

Though they were all somewhat surprised, Peter objected and refused at first to let the Lord wash his feet…only to offer his entire body for washing once Jesus explained that it had to be done.

After the meal, Jesus revealed that someone at the table would betray Him to the authorities; and immediately the shocked disciples "began to question among themselves which of them it might be who would do this" terrible thing.

It was like an echo making its way around the table: "Lord, surely it isn't me?" "Oh surely, Lord, not me?"

And quite soon, things degenerated into an argument "as to which of them was considered to be greatest" of His followers!

Forgetting all about the specter of their Master's betrayal, they began competing with each other about their own faithfulness!

We're not told that Simon Peter was getting loud at this point, but I think he might have been...Because Jesus suddenly speaks specifically to him and warns...

> [31] ... "Simon, Simon, Satan has asked to sift all of you as wheat. [32] But I have prayed for you, Simon, that your faith may not fail. And when you have turned back, strengthen your brothers."
>
> [33] But he replied, "Lord, I am ready to go with you to prison and to death."
>
> [34] Jesus answered, "I tell you, Peter, before the rooster crows today, you will deny three times that you know me."

Peter thought so highly of himself and what he was able to do in his own strength he never considered the possibility of failure — but Jesus did!

Those words of Christ have such a profound effect on my heart.

Do you see how Jesus addresses Peter by his old name again?

Here is the old Simon: competitive, willful, full of self-confidence, sure that He would never let Christ down — so sure that he was "ready to go with (Him) to prison and to death."

But Jesus knows how Satan schemes against those who follow Him.

He knew that "Satan (had) asked to sift all of (them) as wheat" — but especially the headstrong Peter.

Jesus knew that Peter's good intentions were not strong enough to face what was coming and that before dawn broke, Peter would deny knowing Him three times.

But Christ lovingly revealed: "I have prayed for you, Simon, that your faith may not fail."

Christ knew that this would indeed be a terrible test for Peter.

But He also knew that though Peter would fail in this one test, ultimately his faith would not.

He would return; and his new-found humility would enable him to strengthen other believers.

The good news for Peter and for us, is that Christ knows exactly how we are going to be tested and when those tests will come.

And as our Great High Priest, He prays for us.

Many of are familiar with how the story played out …

Later that evening, Judas Iscariot betrayed Christ to the authorities, and Jesus was arrested while at prayer in the Garden of Gethsemane.

All the disciples ran for their lives; and though Peter followed Christ and His captors to the high priest's house he remained outside by the fire in the courtyard, denying that he knew Jesus three times before the rooster crowed, just as Jesus had said.

When he realized what he had done, his heart was filled with crushing defeat. He felt all the emptiness of his earlier bravado.

In the end, he had not had the strength to do what he was so sure he would. And he wept the bitter, sorrowful tears of failure. He watched as Christ, who had no sin, was pronounced guilty. The Lord was stripped, beaten and then nailed to the cross where He died. His body was placed in a tomb.

At that point, I'm sure Peter thought everything he'd committed the last three years of his life to, was over.

But it wasn't! Three days later the faithful women found Christ's tomb was empty…and of course, Peter was the disciple who rushed in to see for himself!

For 40 days, the resurrected Christ met with them, reassuring them, teaching them, and filling them with His Spirit.

Though the disciples were given incredible joy and renewed hope after seeing the Lord alive again, Peter wondered what any of this meant for his future.

After all, he had failed the Lord. He had deserted Jesus and denied knowing Him not once or twice, but three times.

None of the disciples knew exactly what to do next.

And so according to John 21, the fishers of men returned to the Sea of Galilee to fish for fish.

And here, Peter experienced once again the incredible grace of God.

After a long night of effort with nothing but empty nets to show for it, a figure called to them from the shore, suggesting that they would be successful if they changed their strategy.

I'm not sure if they immediately felt how similar this situation was to that day years before when Jesus had first called them to follow Him, but they wearily cast their nets in a new direction and caught so many fish that John recognized the person on the water's edge and cried out "It is the Lord!"

Thankfully, their boat was not far from shore because Peter got so excited he immediately jumped overboard to go to Jesus!

Jesus invited Peter and the others to join Him at a fire He had kindled and served them breakfast.

I can't help but wonder if the fire on the shore that morning reminded Peter of the fire in the high priest's courtyard on the night he'd denied Christ.

It's as if Christ had set the stage for Peter to remember the shameful events of that fateful night, because after their shared meal of fish and bread Jesus began to talk with Peter.

In John 21:15...

> ¹⁵ *When they had finished eating, Jesus said to Simon Peter, "Simon son of John, do you love me more than these?"*

"Yes, Lord," he said, "you know that I love you."

Jesus said, "Feed my lambs."

> ¹⁶ *Again Jesus said, "Simon son of John, do you love me?"*

He answered, "Yes, Lord, you know that I love you."

Jesus said, "Take care of my sheep."

Calling him by his old name Simon, Jesus asks if Peter loves Him.

In the first two questions the Greek word Jesus uses for "love" is "agapao", meaning "to love completely with all that you are as an act of your will".

This is the totally unselfish, unconditional love which is associated with God Himself.

However, Peter responds with a lesser word for love — "philos" from "phileo" meaning: to "love with spontaneous affection or fondness in which emotions play a more prominent role than will".

It is as if each time he was saying: "Yes, Lord; you know I have brotherly affection for You."

I imagine that before his denial of Christ, Peter might have boldly answered Jesus with the word "agape", but He does not do that now, for Peter has been humbled by his failure.

> [17] *The third time (Jesus) said to him, "Simon son of John, do you love me?"*

Peter was hurt because Jesus asked him the third time, "Do you love me?" He said, "Lord, you know all things; you know that I love you."

Jesus said, "Feed my sheep. [18] *Very truly I tell you, when you were younger you dressed yourself and went where you wanted; but when you are old you will stretch out your hands, and someone else will dress you and lead you where you do not want to go."* [19] *Jesus said this to indicate the kind of death by which Peter would glorify God. Then he said to him, "Follow me!"*

Peter is hurt at Christ's repeated question — perhaps not realizing that each question corresponded to one of his denials!

And Christ very graciously gave him a threefold commission.

He told Peter to feed His lambs, to take care of His sheep and to feed His sheep. Of course, Jesus was not really speaking of animals, but rather His flock — His Church!

But do you see that Jesus never asks Peter if he loves the sheep? He only ever asks if Peter loves Him?

Sometimes we think that church leadership falls to those who love the people more – no to be a leader in God's church you really need to love the Shepherd.

The people belong to Him and we are to take care of His flock out of love for Him, even more than out of love for them!

But there is one more thing we should not miss here!

When Jesus asks Peter the third time "Do you love me?"

Jesus changed His word for "love" from "agapao" to match Peter's and He used the word "philos"!

Amazingly, Christ seems to meet Peter where he is!

Christ's final words to Peter are the same as His first so many years before: "Follow me!"

When Peter answered that call in the past, he'd been quite full of himself. He was confident, self-willed, quick to correct the Lord and even object to His directions.

But he is not the same person now. He understands what it means to follow Christ in a much deeper way without pride, without self without his own ideas even if that would take him to martyrdom!

And that is the same call that Jesus speaks to us today!

Have you answered that deeper call? For it is there that we become the followers God had designed us to be, even through our failures?

Peter did become that fisher of men and leader of the Church as Jesus had promised!

He preached the Gospel at Pentecost and 3,000 people were added to their number!

He brought the Gentiles into the Kingdom when he willingly entered the home of the Roman Centurion Cornelius and preached to his entire family.

He faced down the sorcerer Simon; brought the faithful Dorcas back to life; went to believers scattered in the dispersion and left us two epistles in the Scriptures, just to name a few of the ways God used him.

And all of this was ultimately made possible because although he had failed, his faith had not!

He had returned to Christ who by grace, is the God of second chances!

What can we learn from Peter's many encounters with God's grace?…We learn that…

The God of all grace calls us to follow Him, for He sees us not only for who we are, but also for who He wants to make us. That He knows we will be tested; and as our gracious High Priest in heaven, He prays for us. He never leaves us alone in our trials. And because of His amazing grace He is always and forever the God of second chances.

He never gives up on us, but always extends His grace to us when we fall.

Our part is to pick ourselves up and never stop following.

Reflection and Discussion

*P*eter followed Jesus imperfectly, in fits and starts, sometimes getting the point, sometimes not — responding to Christ's gentle and *not-so-gentle* rebukes, receiving His forgiveness and redirection more times than we can count. Through the grace shown to Peter we learn that even in our worst moments, we are not alone and that God is the God of second chances!

Take time to read Luke 5:1-11; Matthew 16:13-18; Luke 22:14:34 and John 21:1-19. Ask God to speak to you through His Word.

- In what ways do you identify with Simon Peter? What words would you use to describe the similarities?

- What spoke to you about Peter's response to Christ's call in Matthew 4 and Luke 5? Do you personally know anyone who has made that kind of life commitment? If so, what have you seen in their life? How does that challenge you personally?

- If you were honest, can you identify anything you have left behind to follow Christ? Or have you realized you're struggling to drag something along with you on the path?

- What did you see in Peter's confession and Christ's response at Caesarea Philippi?

- Why is it so important that we know for ourselves who Christ is and what He is doing?

- How does Christ's declaration that nothing will stand against His Church encourage you? Challenge you?

- Have you ever truly considered that the Lord prays for us as He prayed for Peter? The book of Hebrews reveals Christ is our Great High Priest, interceding for us before God's throne. What difference might this make for us when we are tested?

- Peter was so sure He would never let Christ down and even boasted about his willingness to die for Him. So when he inevitably failed, his defeat was crushing. Is there anything you learn about yourself from his experience?

- Read Romans 8:26-28. What is "the good" that came out of Peter's failures? How was he changed? How did the Lord use him going forward?

- God is indeed the God of second chances. How does this speak to you? Is anyone willing to share about a second chance that God has given you?

- In both the Matthew and John texts, Christ used both of Peter's names in talking to him. Have you ever considered that Christ has a name for you as well — a name that encompasses both who you are and who He wants you to become?

Spend some time praying that you would know His desires for you and that you would allow Him to make you the disciple He longs for you to be.

PAUL

The Power of a Transformed Life

One of the great truths about God is that He makes Himself available to everyone.

No one is beyond the reach of His grace — even His enemies; and nowhere is that better illustrated than in the life of the man who became the great Apostle Paul.

Born in the city of Tarsus, Paul was both a Roman citizen and a wealthy Pharisee.

Paul was his Roman name, Saul his Jewish name.

As a young man, he had been educated at the feet of Rabbi Gamaliel, one of the most prestigious teachers in all Jerusalem.

Paul was a deep thinker, a brilliant and powerful defender of Judaism; and he earned the respect and admiration of the Jewish religious leaders. In fact, he was one of their rising stars.

And in the attempt to eradicate the Church that was rapidly expanding in their midst, he became one of their chief persecutors.

He later described himself as vigorously pursuing believers, throwing them in jail and hunting them even to their deaths.

In fact, we first see him in Scripture guarding the coats of those who stoned the first martyr Stephen to death and the book of Acts tells us he gave full approval to what they did.

He was a committed, driven opponent of this new threat to the Phariseeism he so deeply believed in.

But then Grace intervened.

The risen Lord Himself appeared to Saul on the dusty road to Damascus as he was headed to arrest more believers and the Lord revealed that Saul was really persecuting Him and not just His disciples.

He then told him to go to the city where he would learn what he was supposed to do.

Those who had been travelling with Saul had to lead him by the hand into Damascus as he had been blinded by the light of Christ's presence.

For three days the sightless Saul did not eat or drink while he waited for God's direction.

It was then that God sent His servant Ananias to lay hands on Saul to restore his sight and give him God's message that from now on Saul would be Christ's "chosen instrument to proclaim (the Lord's) name to the Gentiles and their kings and to the people of Israel."

Ananias also warned Saul that there would be much he would suffer as he fulfilled God's call on his life.

And from that moment, grace began to change the Pharisee Saul —enemy and persecutor of the church — into the Apostle Paul — protector of the faith and preacher to the Gentiles.

Paul's encounter with Jesus Christ was dramatically different from others in the New Testament; and his life is filled with so many rich examples of God's grace at work in him and through him. But it seemed fitting to me to look at some things he said about God's grace in his letters.

He wrote 13 of the 27 books of the New Testament, so there is much to draw from. But I've chosen just a few verses to highlight what Paul said about his own life and his own experience of God's grace.

So, where do we begin?

We've already seen that from the time Christ first appeared to him, Paul knew there was a specific call on his life — to preach the Gospel to the Gentiles.

But I think the full dimensions of that call and all it meant became more clear to Paul over time.

Near the end of his life, during one of the many times he spent in prison, he wrote to the church at Ephesus about the nature of his call.

The church there was a mixed congregation, made up of both Jews and Gentiles; and they'd had some struggles with that.

Paul acknowledged that his message may have been hard for Jews there to receive but he confirmed that it had always been God's plan to bring the Gentiles into relationship with

Him as well that both Jew and Gentile were always meant to share together in the forgiveness Christ's death had purchased, and that both would be accepted if they put their faith in Him.

So in Ephesians 3:8 he wrote about how he saw his call and his ministry, saying: "*8 Although I am less than the least of all the Lord's people, this grace was given me: to preach to the Gentiles the boundless riches of Christ …*"

First of all, Paul saw himself as being less than others.

He wasn't boasting. He wasn't arrogant or prideful of what he'd done. On the contrary he acknowledged that the call on his life was a call of GRACE.

God's GRACE made him a chosen vessel for a specific purpose: to take the gospel to the Gentiles.

And you know, it probably hadn't been easy for him to do that.

Have you ever thought he must've had his own reservations about it in the beginning – it was against everything he'd ever been taught for starters.

He'd had some things to think through and overcome.

And following that call had been a hard life physically.

He'd gone to places where others had not gone, taking the Gospel to new areas and new peoples.

He'd met with opposition and misunderstanding. He wound up being persecuted himself.

We will see some more of that later; but here in Ephesians, he could look at it all and say, 'God's grace gave me this to do. And it has been a privilege, a gift.'

And the amazing truth is that God has a grace-filled purpose for your life and mine also!

We, too, are His chosen instruments to proclaim His name to the world we live in today, right where we are.

Now it's quite likely we won't have a ministry as dramatic as Paul's but just as with him, when we have truly believed in Christ, the direction of our life is changed forever.

We no longer live for ourselves, but rather for God's purposes and for His glory.

We have been given a story to tell.

And though our efforts to tell that story are probably simpler than Paul's, they are just as unique and just as vital in God's plan.

And they are just as much a gift of His grace!

Now I know you might be sitting there thinking: "But I'm not as well-qualified as Paul. He was smart, he'd had the best training possible; he was super confident — no wonder God could use him."

But in reality, the second thing we see about GRACE in his life is that it wasn't about his strengths at all. In fact, it was quite the opposite!

If you think about it, this must have been an early realization for Paul because immediately after encountering Christ on the Damascus road, all his "strengths" didn't really matter anymore. With anyone.

His faultless reputation with the Jews was ruined. They wanted nothing to do with him and he wasn't gladly accepted by the Christians either!

Acts 9:26 tells us that Paul "26 ... tried to join the disciples, but they were all afraid of him, not believing that he really was a disciple.

They were suspicious of him and I'm sure we can all understand why.

But God used even this for Paul's eventual benefit because it humbled him.

In a human sense, Paul had a lot of strengths — things he could have taken pride in.

In Philippians 3:4-6 he said, If someone else thinks they have reasons to put confidence in the flesh, I have more: *5 circumcised on the eighth day, of the people of Israel, of the tribe of Benjamin, a Hebrew of Hebrews; in regard to the law, a Pharisee; 6 as for zeal, persecuting the church; as for righteousness based on the law, faultless.*

But he had learned something in the years that followed that Damascus road experience!

Listen to what he says in the very next verses:

> *7 But whatever were gains to me I now consider loss for the sake of Christ. 8 What is more, I consider everything a loss because of the surpassing worth of knowing Christ Jesus my Lord, for whose sake I have lost all things. I consider them garbage, that I may gain Christ 9 and be found in him, not having a righteousness of my own that comes from the law, but that which*

is through faith in[a] Christ—the righteousness that comes from God on the basis of faith.

Paul came to understand that everything he'd had and everything he'd been was worthless compared with what He'd received in Christ.

And I think the good news for all of us in that, is that the King of Glory really doesn't need what we can bring to the table either…

He uses whomever He chooses to use, and sends them out with His unlimited and unconditional grace and when you realize that, it IS humbling.

Apparently, humility was something Paul needed to be refreshed on, for God gave him a recurring reminder of his own weaknesses lest he begin again to think more highly of himself than he ought.

Paul called it a "thorn in the flesh."

We don't know what type of hardship or irritant this "thorn" was, but Paul clearly knew God gave it to him; and its purpose was to keep him dependent on the Lord.

In 2 Corinthians 12:7-10 he explains that he pleaded with the Lord three times for it to be removed. but God had answered…

⁹ … *"My grace is sufficient for you, for My strength is made perfect in weakness."*

Whatever the thorn was, it wasn't as important as what it accomplished.

It kept Paul's eyes firmly focused on God. It kept him dependent on God's grace, and it gave an opportunity for God's strength to be made manifest.

So much so that ultimately Paul came to see it as a blessing, realizing that "when (he was) weak" Christ's power and God's faithfulness were even more evident.

Paul learned that God's Grace transforms our weaknesses into blessings.

GRACE also taught Paul something else very important.

It taught him to be content in whatever circumstances he faced.

When he wrote from prison to the church at Philippi he assured them in Philippians 1:12...

¹²Now I want you to know, brothers, that what has happened to me has really served to advance the Gospel ...."

He believed that even being imprisoned and chained to a Roman soldier had its uses because it gave him a captive audience!

And many of those soldiers he shared the good news of Christ with became believers!

Paul was using his chains to advance the Gospel!

And in Philippians 4:12-13 Paul let them in on the reason he could live so confidently and peacefully in those chains. It was because he had...

12 ... learned the secret of being content in any and every situation, whether well fed or hungry, whether living in plenty or in want.13 (He said) I can do all this through him who gives me strength.

Paul knew that even in the most adverse situations, God was with him!

And in an even later letter, written to his son in the faith, Timothy, he said in 2 Timothy 4:17 that in his darkest moments: " ... (the) Lord stood at my side and gave me strength, so that through me the message might be fully proclaimed and all the Gentiles might hear it..."

Make no mistake — Paul had a difficult life as a follower of Christ; and there really were many other things besides chains and imprisonment that "happened to him" as he followed Jesus.

Conveniently for us, he listed some of those things in 2 Corinthians 11:24-28...

24 Five times I received from the Jews the forty lashes minus one. 25 Three times I was beaten with rods, once I was pelted with stones, three times I was shipwrecked, I spent a night and a day in the open sea, 26 I have been constantly on the move. I have been in danger from rivers, in danger from bandits, in danger from my fellow Jews, in danger from Gentiles; in danger in the city, in danger in the country, in danger at sea; and in danger from false believers. 27 I have labored and toiled and have often gone without sleep; I have known hunger and thirst and have often gone without food; I have been cold and naked. 28 Besides everything else, I face daily the pressure of my concern for all the churches.

How did he endure all that?

It was because he had learned to be content in every circumstance, and he knew that he could do all things through Christ who gave him strength!

Paul didn't directly relate this next point to the working of grace in his life, but I think it abundantly clear that that was the source.

I want us to see something that only grace could enable him to say!

In 1 Corinthians 11:1 he said...

¹ Follow my example, as I follow the example of Christ.

He gave this same challenge to the believers in Philippi, but in an expanded way.

In Philippians 4 he first encouraged them to do some specific things:

⁴ Rejoice in the Lord always. I will say it again: Rejoice! ⁵ Let your gentleness be evident to all. The Lord is near. ⁶ Do not be anxious about anything, but in every situation, by prayer and petition, with thanksgiving, present your requests to God. ⁷ And the peace of God, which transcends all understanding, will guard your hearts and your minds in Christ Jesus.

⁸ Finally, brothers and sisters, whatever is true, whatever is noble, whatever is right, whatever is pure, whatever is lovely, whatever is admirable—if any-thing is excellent or praiseworthy—think about such things.

And then he told them in verse 9 —

⁹ Whatever you have learned or received or heard from me, or seen in me—put it into practice. And the God of peace will be with you.

Empowered by the Holy Spirit, Paul followed Christ wholeheartedly, and he confidently called others to follow in his steps because he knew where that path ended: with Christ Himself!

He mentioned several specific actions and attitudes the Philippians should have in their lives and he promised that all who would do these things as he himself had done, would find the same peace he had known.

I don't know about you, but that is a real challenge to me.

We often say jokingly, "Do as I say, not as I do."

But Paul said, "Do as I do. It will take you to the right place."

Only a grace-filled life could offer itself as that kind of example.

There was another way in which Paul was an example to us. He not only showed us how to follow Christ, he showed us how to finish well!

In Acts 21 Luke reveals that on his final journey to Jeru-salem before his arrest, Paul was warned by a prophet named

Agabus that he would be bound and delivered to the Gentiles.

When those accompanying Paul heard this, they begged him not to go.

Acts 21:13-14 reveal Paul's reply...

> *¹³ Then Paul answered, "Why are you weeping and breaking my heart? I am ready not only to be bound, but also to die in Jerusalem for the name of the Lord Jesus." ¹⁴ When he would not be dissuaded, we gave up and said, "The Lord's will be done."*

Paul was ready to make any sacrifice necessary for the Lord, even if that meant he was to die for the name of the Lord Jesus.

And the prophecy proved to be true.

Paul was arrested in Jerusalem and spent many years in Roman prisons after that.

He would be released, only to be arrested again around 67AD; and this time, according to tradition, he was beheaded in Rome, suffering the customary means of death for a Roman citizen.

During that final imprisonment shortly before his death, in the same letter to Timothy we referenced earlier, he wrote ...

> *⁶ For I am already being poured out like a drink offering, and the time for my departure is near. ⁷ I have fought the good fight, I have finished the race, I have kept the faith. ⁸ Now there is in store for me the crown of righteousness, which the Lord, the righteous Judge, will award to me on that day—and not only to me, but also to all who have longed for his appearing.*

Michele Telfer

Confined to prison and facing imminent death, Paul looked back on his life with a sense of peace and completion. He had fought well.

He had finished what had been set before him and most importantly of all, he had kept the faith.

He was ready to meet the Lord. And he was confident of receiving the reward God gives to all who long for His appearing — the crown of righteousness!

I wonder if we can say the same things Paul did?

Are we depending on God in every situation? Are we content with where He has placed us for now?

Do we model faith as Paul did? Do we dare ask others to follow us as we follow Christ?

Are we confident in the face of death that we have given everything we have to serve Him?

Paul's life reveals so much about God's grace.

By grace God gave Paul a purpose as His chosen instrument to take the news of Jesus Christ to others and it was Grace that helped him to experience God's power through his weaknesses rather than his strengths.

Grace enabled Paul to do all things through Christ's strength and be content in whatever circumstances he faced.

And grace empowered him to be an example to others as he fought the good fight, as he finished the race and kept the faith in order to finish well!

And that same grace is available for us in the Lord Jesus Christ.

Will we turn to Him?

Will we follow Him?

Will we finish the course He has laid out for each one of us?

We can, through grace and grace alone.

In these past chapters, we have studied some remarkable people and learned how encountering God's grace in Christ changed their lives.

Nicodemus showed us how ...

God's grace receives us just as we are ...

It speaks truth to us in ways that we can understand.

But grace is personal – it requires our response, our personal faith in Christ's sacrifice.

The Samaritan woman's encounter with Jesus at the well of Sychar revealed that by grace.

God sees every soul as valuable. He is seeking out every one of us, no matter who we are or what we've been.

By grace He helps us to see ourselves as we really are, and it is there that we are made whole because once things are exposed, things can be healed.

And finally, the grace of God in Christ sets us free to share with others! We too, can work in His fields and bring in the harvest He so desires.

John the Baptist encouraged us with the truth that ...

The grace of God sets us apart even before we are born and unfolds God's plan to us as we walk in obedience to His call.

Grace encourages us and gives us the strength to hold on even when we doubt.

And yes, it is the grace of God that enables us to fulfill our ministry and to finally hear those words from our Lord: "Well done, good and faithful servant".

The dear sisters of Lazarus brought us comfort as we learned that...

Grace is at work even when our world is shattered and it seems as if God doesn't care, His love for us is never in question.

This physical life we so desperately cling to is not the whole story because it is only temporary — for God by His grace has provided eternal life to those who believe in Jesus Christ for He is the life and the resurrection we all so desperately need.

Grace feels our pain and God is moved by our suffering. He weeps with us, but more than that He invites us to join Him in the work that only He can do, removing obstacles that keep people from believing and helping each other lay aside the things that bind us and keep us from following Him.

Beloved Peter helped us to understand that …

The God of all grace calls us to follow Him, and that He sees us not only for who we are, but also for who He wants to make us.

He knows we will be tested; and as our gracious High Priest in heaven, He prays for us. He never leaves us alone in our trials.

And because of his amazing grace He is always and forever the God of second chances.

He never gives up on us, but always extends His grace to us when we fall.

Our part is to pick ourselves up and never stop following.

And finally, the great Apostle Paul showed us that no one is beyond God's grace. He can reach all those who are far from Him — even His enemies! And that …

God has a grace-filled purpose for our lives as we are His chosen instruments to proclaim His name to others and Grace will help us to experience God's power in our weaknesses rather than our strengths.

And as we learn to find contentment in whatever circumstances we face, Christ's grace will enable us to do all things in the strength He gives us.

And we will be able to be an example to others as we fight the good fight, finish the race and keep the faith.

Because of God's grace in Jesus Christ. we will be able to finish well as we keep our eyes firmly fixed on Him!

My prayer for us all as we end our study is what Peter wrote in 2 Peter 3:17-18:

> [17] *Therefore, dear friends, since you have been fore-warned, be on your guard so that you may not be carried away by the error of the lawless and fall from your secure position.* [18] *But grow in the grace and knowledge of our Lord and Savior Jesus Christ. To him be glory both now and forever! Amen.*

Reflection and Discussion

We conclude our study with Paul, whose life was completely transformed by his encounters with the grace of Jesus Christ. A grace so powerful that it was able to change the Pharisee Saul — enemy and persecutor of the Church —into the Apostle Paul — protector of the faith and preacher to the Gentiles.

Take time to read Acts 9:1-30; Philippians 3:4-9; Philippians 4:4-9 and 4:12-13; and 2 Corinthians 11:24-28. Ask God to speak to you through His Word.

- Were there any ways in which Paul reminded you of Peter? How would you say they differed? What do you think that says about how God works and who He uses?

- What things do you think stood in the way of Paul coming to believe in Christ?

- How did his dramatic conversion In Acts 9:1-30 speak to you?

- God made His purpose for Paul clear from the very beginning. He didn't have to ask or wonder what God wanted him to do. But it doesn't always happen that way for most of us. At this point in your life, could you describe what you feel His purpose for you is? If you're not sure, how might you go about discerning that?

- In Ephesians 3:8, Paul characterized the ministry God had given him as a "grace." In other words, an undeserved gift. What ministries has God given you? How are you treating them?

- Paul had so many things to be proud of in the world's eyes; and yet nothing was as important to him as what he found in Christ. It seems that Paul didn't just add Jesus on to who he was and what he did ... rather he completely refocused his life on serving Jesus. How has Christ transformed the way that you live, the things you trust in, the goals you pursue, etc. Is this still a struggle for you?

- Has God ever allowed a "thorn in the flesh" in your life — something that keeps you dependent on him? It doesn't have to be an actual physical issue. It can be a person or a particular circumstance you have trouble with. How has your struggle taught you to rely on His strength? Have you seen His strength revealed to others by how you handle things?

- Philippians 4:12-13 reveals that Paul had *learned* to be content in every situation. Contentment doesn't come naturally to the heart of man. We are naturally ambitious, acquisitive and sadly, even jealous. How do you see this in the world around us? How would you define "contentment"? Does being content mean that you do nothing to improve your situation?

- What do you think "contentment" looked like to Paul in prison?

- What gave Paul the confidence to ask others to follow him?

- Think back through Paul's life. How does he show us to follow Christ? What are some of the footsteps he has left for us?

- In what ways would you say you are a good example to others? Does that mean living a life of perfection? How do you respond to your own weaknesses? How can you use them to glorify God's grace?

- What would "finishing the race" look like to you? What legacy do you want to leave? How can you begin to live that way today?

Spend some time praying that you would follow him wholeheartedly and that, like Paul, you would finish well.

ABOUT MICHELE

*B*orn to non-Christian parents in Zambia, Africa, Michele grew up in the neighboring country of Zimbabwe. It was there that she met her husband-to-be, Colin; and the couple were married in 1983. During their first year of marriage, Michele and Colin relocated to Botswana, another nation in southern Africa. It was there—after living a life far from God—that they both became totally committed followers of Jesus. During their 16 years in Botswana, the Telfers frequently went on Safari, often traveling by themselves through vast tracts of wilderness.

Michele first began teaching the Bible in Botswana, with invitations to teach coming one after the other, often in unusual ways. When she and Colin moved to the U.S. in 1999, the Lord opened up many opportunities in their new homeland (the Telfers subsequently became U.S. citizens). Within a few years, Michele was teaching multiple groups of eager students of the Word in Southern California. Invitations started to come in from around the globe, leading to speaking engagements in places across Africa, Australia, Canada, the U.K., and other parts of the U.S. Michele now lives in Arkansas but continues to present weekly Bible classes online and speaks to groups across America and around the world. She also has a very large radio ministry across Africa and the Middle East, where her Bible classes are broadcast weekly.

Michele Telfer Ministries is devoted to communicating the two greatest realities of all—the Living Word of God, Jesus Christ, and the Written Word of God, the Bible. Her material can be accessed online at www.intheword.com. To us, "In The Word" means being in Him and living in His Truth. All resources published and distributed by In the Word are designed to guide and encourage students as they "grow in the grace and knowledge of our Lord and Savior Jesus Christ" (2 Peter 3:18). To connect with us online visit www.InTheWord.com or scan the QR code below:

www.ingramcontent.com/pod-product-compliance
Lightning Source LLC
LaVergne TN
LVHW041213080426
835508LV00011B/935